To Ariel,

The
Bowery Bartenders
Big Book of Poems

So Nice
to see
you. Shit
on my FACE
lesbo. Keepw

keep.w in
Love
Love. Mooren

The
Bowery Bartenders
Big Book of Poems

Shappy
Moonshine Shorey
Laurel Barclay
Gary Mex Glazner

BOWERY POETRY SERIES #2
Bob Holman, PUBLISHER

YBK Publishers, New York

The Bowery Bartenders Book of Poetry

YBK Publishers, Inc.
425 Broome St.
New York, NY 10013

ISBN 0-9764359-2-6

Library of Congress Control Number: 2005932831

Manufactured in the United States of America

Ver 05-09

Poems by Laurel Barclay on pages 65–91; by Gary Glazner on pages
94–123; by Moonshine Shorey on pages 32-63; by Shappy on pages
5–28 appear with permission of the authors

Cover and Interior Photographers: Lina Pallotta (Shappy,
Moonshine Shorey); Neil Selkirk (Laurel Barclay); Reid Yalom
(Gary Mex Glazner)

Bowery Poetry Books is the imprint of
Bowery Arts & Science, Ltd.,
a 501(c) (3) nonprofit cultural organization,
and are published in affiliation with YBK Publishers, Inc.,
whose publisher, Otto Barz, is the inspiration for this series.
With thanks to Bill Adler.

Contents

28 Footnotes in Search of a Drink   vii

Bowery Poetry Club Signature Drinks   xiv

Shappy   2

Moonshine Shorey   30

Laurel Barclay   62

Gary Mex Glazner   92

28 Footnotes in Search of a Drink

Bob's Intro to TBBBBOP

Start with the premise that if you have the audacity to open a poetry bar[1] these days[2] the bartenders might as well be poets—support the art by providing a poet a salary so that the rent gets paid and the poems writ. Blend in my years of nonprofit poetry work with CETA[3], NYC PoCal,[4] St. Mark's,[5] Nuyorican[6]—boy, do I know

---

1 They say you'll never go broke running a bar in New York. We at the Bowery Poetry Club are giving it a try.

2 The Horrific Triumph of Capitalism.

3 Yup, I worked at all these anti-institutions! The Comprehensive Employment and Training Act was Jimmy Carter's attempt at a last-ditch program to train the terminally unemployed on how to enter the work force. That was sure me in 1977. And a lot of other artists, too—the CETA Artists project threw 350 of us together to show that artists could be useful and it worked (so long as the government picked up the tab). At the time, I was too embarrassed to even acknowledge I was working for the Feds (this was just post-Vietnam); now, I'm gung-ho for governmental engagement with the arts. For one thing I met a heap of great artists from all disciplines—Pedro Pietri, Dana Reitz, Marc Levin to name a few.

4 Sara Miles, Susie Timmons and I started the free monthly broadside *NYC Poetry Calendar* in 1977 so that the community could find all the readings in one spot, so that all the poets could be on the same page. Most recently it can be found at Jackie Sheeler's poetz.com and on the back cover of David Kirschenbaum's newsprint poetry news, *Boog City*.

5 The St. Mark's Poetry Project, founded in 1966, is still one of the most active artist-run art centers in the world. I worked there first running the Monday Series (1977–80) and then as Coordinator with

how not to make a profit!—as well as my days as a singing
bartender/waiter at Your Father's Moustache with their
banjo band.[7] Add a dash of Ed Greer,[8] *Guru du Bar,* who
managed the Knitting Factory for a dozen years before
realizing that the *real* challenge was harnessing a poetic
economy in real time—without Ed, how would a poet
like I face a business like the Club? Next, stir in the
entire history of the Bowery[9] as a site for populist enter-
tainment, habitat of the down and in. Mix with the
dynamics of change and gentrification and some stalwart

Bernadette Mayer as Director, '80–'84. I wrote press releases every
week. It was like tossing paper airplanes into the abyss. During these
years the Project institutionalized itself, a horrific experience that I've
also lived through with the Nuyorican and the Poetry Slam.

6 The Nuyorican Poets Café, where I worked from '88–'96. The Café
was founded in the mid-'70s by Miguel Algarin, Miguel Piñero, Lucky
CienFuegos and others. The Café was closed '82–'89; I helped reopen
it then, at which point the Future barged through the door, wow.
Aloud! (Holt, 1995), which Algarin and I edited (now in its sixteenth
printing) came from that. So did *Slam*—the event, the book, the
movie; the touring company; a record label; the reading series at Fez;
the whole megillah! Which is from where I carry on now at BPC.

7 I made my first TV appearances (Ed Sullivan, Mike Douglas) with
the banjo band; sneaked out of student-occupied buildings at
Columbia in '68 to make my shifts; and thus began my life in the bar
business at the Moustache on the corner at 10th Street and Seventh
Avenue ('68–'70). Shouts to Keith Ramsdale and Joel Schiavone.

8 Pride of Ballycastle!

9 ". . . the Bowery always possessed the greatest number of grog-
geries, flophouses, clip joints, brothels, fire sales, rigged auctions,
pawnbrokers, dime museums, shooting galleries, dime-a-dance estab-
lishments, fortune-telling agencies, lottery agencies, thieves' markets,
and tattoo parlors, as well as theaters of the second, third, fifth and
tenth rank. It is also a fact that the Bowery is the only major thorough-
fare in New York never to have had a single church built upon it."
from *Low Life,* Luc Sante.

artists who want an anchor for the Lower East Side's everchanging artistic history.[10] Let flow eternally.

The result is in your hands: *The Bowery Bartenders Big Book of Poems*.

So this anthology brings you four poets[11] whose common ground is the apple ply bar[12] at 308 Bowery, site of the Bowery Poetry Club, *Serving the World Poetry Since 2002*. I'd thought at first that we should have an old, burnished, bourbon-and-a-beer-back bar; I even called across the street to Kate Millett[13] at what was formerly McGurk's Suicide Hall[14] to see if that bar was still around somewhere. But the lighter and brighter, 2000 Era bar we got is more to our spirits. And behind the bar (and sometimes on it) stand these four poets slash barkeeps.

---

10 The BPC stands with the Federation of East Village Artists in relishing the dynamism of the most variegated community on earth: poetry readings, perfs, and slams, art battles, hip-hop, music, dance, paint 'n sculpt, film, video, and drama by cultural icons and up-and-comers alike have all found a home in the double Dutch Colonial building. Numerous events happen every day; for a complete list, see the calendar on the website (www.bowerypoetry.com) or call 212.614.0505.

11 After Corinth Press's *Four Young Lady Poets* (Carol Berge, Barbara Moraff, Rochelle Owens, Diane Wakoski). Edited by LeRoi Jones in 1962.

12 Bar design by Alex Kraft and built by Brian Papa and the gang at Made.

13 Kate, Mother of Feminism, was a wonderful, cantankerous neighbor till she finally was bought out for the Avalon Chrystie Place Development new neighborhood. She'd drop by to chat and have a sugar cookie or two at the café.

14 295 Bowery. Working conditions at "the roughest bar in town" were so horrible (you bought beer by the minute and were handed the hose) that five backroom girls drank carbolic acid in a rare group suicide. Demolished, July 11, 2005.

While said bartenders generally don't accept poems as legal tender,[15,16] they will, on occasion, offer you a poem as change[17], or, for no particular reason. Sometimes from atop the bar,[18] with or without spotlight.[19] Sometimes as part of a poetry slam, sometimes as part of a radio show,[20] in which the whole Club is the studio. All four are excellent mixologists—in fact, Gary's poems double as actual recipes. But it ain't just about the booze. It's all about the Poetry. And while applying for a job at the Club is different from applying to an MFA Writing Program,[21] it has become apparent that some terrific writers are being drawn to

---

15 This phrase brings up all kinds of questions, starting with what "legal" and "tender" mean. Also, how do you live in a poetic economy in an anti-poetic age? Also, how does a poet earn a living any time, anyway?

16 There are exceptions: to find out how to trade a poem for a drink drop by 308 Bowery and query the bartender.

17 Whatever that means! Currently, our sign painter Mark Turgeon has writ "Everything Is Subject To Change" above the BPC entrance. George McKibbens, our door, will point to this whenever there is a conflict between what's at www.bowerypoetry.com and what is actually going on on stage.

18 This perch was pioneered by Moonshine, who at 6'3" and 250 presents quite the imposing silhouette up there. Check his grace as he descends.

19 Shouts out here to the extraordinary Tech Crew at the BPC: Sascha von Oertzen, our director, and Stefan Zeniuk, Misha Volf, Kris Anton, Sean T. Hanratty, Derrick Bernard, all of whom effortlessly swizzle the spot round to hit the barkeep.

20 "Live from the Bowery Poetry Club!" is in the pre-stage right now but has had several performances gearing up for the big ears of radio. Jocelyn Gonzalez is producing, Ed Greer is The Voice of Reason, I host, and we're indebted to Dean Capello and Stacy Abramson at WNYC radio for support. Keep your ears tuned—poetry radio is nigh!

21 I should know. I've taught at The New School and Bard, and for the best several years I've taught "Exploding Text: Poetry Performance" at Columbia University School of the Arts. Shouts to Alan Ziegler.

this little old utopian experiment in art and community[22].

We got Shappy, who moved to New York from his beloved Chicago to run the bar, leaving his run as whacko host of readings, agent-provocateur of Quimby's Books, and oft-times cohost of the high-larious rantings of shockjock Mancow. Here he comperes the bar like it's a burlesque hall, mixing drinks with one hand—microphone in the other. Every Tuesday at midnight it's Night Cap with Shap (drunk ranters welcome!) when an Open Mic intermingles with Shappy's collection of Star Wars rarities and other nerd phenomena. Shappy! Funniest poet on the block! And there are over 5,000 poets on this block. And every Thursday he creates the Impossible— he holds down his job as bartender while hosting the Urbana Poetry Slam! [23] You gotta see it![24]

Moonshine's entry into the Club has become apocryphal. Hire me, said this big beautiful galoot, I'll work for free. Got my attention, got him a job, and now not only is he Downtown Ingénue of the year but also runs his own "closed mic" (you don't read till he says so) on Wednesday midnights. When he stands on the bar he disappears into the top shelf booze, as his poems of trailer parks and white trash sushi disappear the crowd

---

22 Here's where I get to mention Black Mountain College, and Vincent Katz's great book, *Black Mountain: Experiment in Art* (MIT Press: 2003).

23 When Urbana (BPC's slam team) Slammasters Taylor Mali and Cristin O'Keefe Aptowicz handed Shappy the reins as Host, who knew that work and art could be so thoroughly intertwined? Shappy! That's who! Drop by to see the weekly show—check www.bowerypoetry.com for schedule and www.uncleshappy.com to rap with Shap.

24 Six bucks.

into a haze of memory and diesel fuel. Check calendar for his variety show, "Moony's Spooky Trailer," and appearenaces as the tranny Ginger in Jennifer Blowdryer's[25] "White Trash Debutante."

Laurel Barclay first came my way as a high school student at City as School taking *Exploding Text* at The New School. Her poems then as now are pure rock'n'roll condensed in a breathtakingly commanding way. When I moved to Bard to teach, there she was, and I was soon overseeing the book of poems that was her senior thesis and would become the basis of her section in this book. So it was only natural that she would graduate to being a bartender at the Bowery Poetry Club, where her band *Daddy* was the first house band. In the tradition of Lou Reed, Patti Smith, Jim Carroll,[26] here's your rock'n'roll angel, here's Laurel Barclay!

Gary Glazner and I go 'way back to a Poets Theater Workshop I led in San Francisco in the '70s. He took to the New poetry (i.e., post-Homer) with verve verbs—he is, after all The Official Minister of Fun of Poetry Slam International, and author of *Poetry Slam: The Competitive Art of Performance Poetry* and *How to Make a Living As a Poet* which includes a chapter on his life as Manager of BPC back in the summer of '02, when he and George Tysh[27] took over for me for the month of August. Gary's drink recipes are the perfectly balanced

---

25 If only Jennifer were a bartender!

26 No footnote could do justice. The Club hereby swears to do a book of these heroes' verses as soon as we work out the contractual essences.

27 Tysh is Poet Laureate of Detroit—IMHO. A great laid-back poet, philosopher, zen monk activist.

metaphor between art and commerce, aestheticism and revelry. Sure, many of these drinks can be made at home, but they can ALL be found at the Bowery Poetry Club.

Never mix, never worry—so they say. Well, poetry is supposed to make you worry, a little bit anyway, so, you there, belly up to the bar of the Bowery Poetry Club and say ahhhhhhhhhhhhh. . . .[28]

Cheers!

Bob Holman
New York
September, 2005

---

[28] These words suggested as opening for this introduction by old college chum, John Surgal, who, coincidentally, was sitting on the Stuart Hanlon Memorial Bar Stool. Stu, also veteran of the Columbia Wars, was the only human being I could convince to invest in a poetry club.

Bowery Poetry Club Signature Drinks

These five drinks were developed by Shappy, Moonshine, and Laurel, and are available at the BPC. We hope they conjure the spirits of poesy for ye!

Moony's Gay-Dar Aid
1/2 oz Raspberry vodka   1/2 oz Blue Curaçao
1/2 oz Peach schnapps   Pineapple juice
Sprite   Splash of Midori

Lovingly layer the liquor, then rhumba with the juice. Fizzy it up with Sprite, splash the Midori, garnish with my true love's stare—one sip and you'll *KNOW!*

The Shapple
3 counts Cranberry Stoli   Ginger ale
3 counts Apple schnapps   Maraschino cherry

Better than an apple martooni!

Walt's Leaves of Grasshopper
1 oz Vanilla Stoli   1/2 oz Crème de cacao
1/2 oz green Crème de menthe   Milk (or cream)

After Whitman drank these he began to sing
And they were songs of himself!

The Allen Gin-sberg
Howl in some grenadine   Impish Sprite
Gin! Gin! Gin!   Maraschino cherry
Top with Blue Curaçao

I saw the best minds of my generation. . .

The Pukowski
One PBR
One shot house whiskey

The
Bowery Bartenders
Big Book of Poems

Shappy

Shappy has always had a fascination with obscure cartoon characters. Perhaps it is because he *is* an obscure cartoon character.

Called "The most purely comic poet in the scene" by About.com, Shappy has left many a poetry audience soaked in chuckle sauce since first entering the Chicago scene in the early 90s. His success in slam during those early Green Mill days led to him being the first poet ever bleeped by CNN (they were reporting on this "new slam phenomenon"), one of the first poets to co-host MTV's "120 Minutes" as well, leading to Shappy touring with Lollapalooza's Spoken Word Revival Tent in 1994. Despite Shappy spending several months on the road with Lollapalooza, hosting and performing with such acts as the Beastie Boys, Billy Corrigan and L7, BPC owner Bob Holman can only *seem* to remember Shappy's Lollapalooza contribution as being the one time he caused frat boys to put on dresses and run around while balancing cherries on their bums, tossing them into a cup for a chance to win a free t-shirt—which Shap poetically called "Drag Racing." (Shap would like to assure Bob, now his boss, that was a one-time only thing . . . and that it was indeed hilarious.)

With the Lollapalooza tour and his "Drag Racing" days behind him, Shap continues to blaze the scene with his unique and hilarious poetry, performing at such acclaimed venues as South By Southwest, Second City and several Chicago Comedy Festivals.

Although Shap was a long-time slammer and had attended many National Poetry Slams (mostly as a "Shap-erone" for the various Austin teams), he never competed on a team until the 2000 Providence Nationals, where he not only won the heart of his current gal pal, Cristin O'Keefe Aptowicz, but also found himself in the individual semifinals where his electric performances garnered an invitation to perform in Denmark. A word of advice to poets looking to perform in Denmark—Susan Lucci jokes will go COMPLETELY over the heads of Denmarkians. However, their appreciation of karaoke more than makes up for it.

After ten years in Chicago (and a year-long, pet-name-filled, long-distance courtship with Cristin), Shap finally made the leap to New York City. Since then, Shappy has won a National Slam Championship, produced two books of poetry and has appeared on

HBO's "Def Poetry Jam." A BPC bartender and manager from opening day, Shap is now as much a fixture there as the $3 Pabst Blue Ribbon specials. You can find him behind the bar or hosting Urbana on Thursdays, Nitecap with Shap on Tuesdays, and drinking with his New York pals on any given night!

Shappy enjoys vintage pop culture memorabilia, candy of all varieties, and laughing at Khan's superior intellect. Shappy currently resides with Cristin in Astoria, Queens, where they dream of one day starting a rock band/detective agency consisting only of wiener dogs. Need more information to satisfy your Shappy fetish? Get yourself over to www.uncleshappy.com, where you will be treated to videos, mp3s, photos, a mom-friendly blog and contact information for booking Shap for performances.

Shappy would like to thank: John and Brenda Seasholtz, Cal & Katie & Luke & Taylor Seasholtz; the BPC crew especially Papa Matt Lydon (for keeping him in line), Moonie for being such a great co-worker/drinking buddy; Ernie Cline for being the R2D2 to Shap's gay C3PO; Juliette and Sam Henderson for his award-winning Kapow! books ("Sensitive Little Poetry Boy," "Little Book of ASS" and "I Hate ALL Wars [Except for STAR WARS]"); Poppa Holman for everything he has done (including this tome); and Cristin O'Keefe Aptowicz for providing all the joy and love a growing Shappy needs.

AMERICA!

Make no mistake!

I want to hug the shit out of you!

I want to embrace you like Travolta embraces
      Dianetics.

I want to nibble on your ear and breathe hotly down
      your neck
Until your patriotic poonani pulsates with pleasure!

You are a hot slut, America.
You are a sweet tart, America.

I weep openly in your candy aisles.
Your variety is overwhelming.

America, I want to see all your sights, all of your
      roadside attractions.
Fill my knick-knack shelf with your self-effacing
      CUTENESS!
Who's a cute lil' country, huh? Who's a cute lil' country?
Oh, America, you are soooooooooooooooo CUTE!

And I want to see you NAKED!
Take it off, America!
Show us your tits, America!
Go wild on Spring Break, America!
You love it when I talk dirty to you, America!
You love it when I pinch your bountiful ass, America!
Every night and every day, we're cumming on America!
And wiping it off with your flag, America!

You wanna be my fuck buddy?
I guess that's okay by me, America.
You just don't want to get to know me, America.
You don't even want my cellphone number, America.
Have your way with me, America.
Let's roll, America.
I did not have sexual relations with that America!

I want more from you but I know you're busy, America.

America
When will you love me
As much as I hate myself
For loving you
AMERICA!

NOT WITHOUT MY GODDAMN BABIES, GODDAMN IT!

When the soldiers came to my village

And took my babies

I shook my fist, like this, and yelled

"BRING BACK MY BABIES! YOU SOLDIERS OF
        THIS GODDAMN WAR!"
This WAR that pits brother against brother

Sister against mother

And that one guy against that other guy, you know that
        guy with the mustache and the Battlestar
        Galactica t-shirt?

THAT guy!
THIS war!
THOSE soldiers!
MY babies!

I was feeding my babies wax beans that I grew in the
        walls of our shoddy shanty made
Of shit and mud.

Look at your hands! Are they brown like mine?

We were a proud family, my babies and I.
Until the soldiers came and took my babies!

Who are these soldiers?

So brave.
So bold
So beautiful

WHO ARE THEY? AND WHY DID THEY TAKE MY BABIES?

I moved to this village because I was led to believe that
    this was the sort of village where
Soldiers would NOT take your babies! I'm going to give
    that realtor a piece of my mind!
I should at least get my finder's fee back!

Oh well, I suppose now I'll have to get some more
    babies.

Some babies that soldiers will NOT want to take!

ALL AMERICAN A-HOLE

Hello, everyone!

I'm an asshole!

I'm sorry, did I say asshole?

I meant to say white American male!

I eat at McDonald's and I just saw *Men In Black 2*!

Boy, that movie was funny!

It had Micheal Jackson in it.

He is a good singer.

I have all of his albums including his latest one which is
    awesome!

I also support the President who is a good president
    who is smart and

Brave and honest.

I voted for him twice!

You can tell I love America because I am wearing
    a t-shirt with an

American flag on it.

See it?

That means I am patriotic.

I can't believe they took "under God" out of the

Pledge of America!

Now when I say the pledge I say UNDER GOD really
    loud so

President Bush and Jesus can hear me and know that I
    am

PROUD to live in a country where I can buy as much

PORNOGRAPHY AND FIREARMS AS I WANT!

Because I love BASEBALL and TALK RADIO and
    watching

SURVIVOR! Sometimes after I watch SURVIVOR! I go
    on

AMERICA ON LINE and talk about it on the inter-web.

Some people in the world hate Americans like me
    because they are
JEALOUS.
Well, I hope those people stay far away from me
    because I'll tell them to
KISS MY BIG, WHITE, HAIRY, AMERICAN BUTT!
    HAW!
That'll show Omar Ben Kenobi!
Well, it was nice talking to you, but, now I gotta get in
    my SUV,
Call my buddies on my cellular telephone and get my
    kid the new HARRY POTTER
At the shopping mall.
Hey, God bless America . . . UNDER GOD!!!

NEW THINGS

I enjoy new things.
In fact, the newer they are, the more I enjoy them!
When I was a kid I enjoyed playing my Atari 2600
    (when it was new)
But now I say "Fuck that shit!"
Put that old shit on a t-shirt and sell it to a college
    student!
Now I enjoy playing hyper-realistic games on a compact
    disc that
I put in my X-BOX.
It is the newest in technology.
Have you played the video game in which you are
    skateboarding in
OUTER SPACE?
I played it for 5 hours yesterday.
I would like to see a movie based on that video game.
But only if they come up with some new computer
    generated imagery
Like they did in that movie *The Scorpion King* starring
    The Rock.
The Rock was the new action hero until "XXX" came
    out and then
Vin Diesel became the new action hero.
Perhaps Vin Diesel could star in a movie about
    skateboarding in outer space!
That would be AWESOME!
I also enjoy new beverages.
I enjoy the new Vanilla Coke and the Mountain Dew
    Red and the Pepsi Blue.
I like these beverages because they have new colors and
    new colors make the
Soda taste better and, of course, newer!

I enjoy new television shows that are watched by other
        people first so that
I will know which ones to watch.
I can't wait for the new season of Survivor!
Wait, that's not new anymore.
I can't wait for the new American Idol!
That's a great new show and it produced a new singing
        sensation
Kelly What's-her-face!
She and Justin Big Hair sang new songs that I enjoyed
        very much because
I had never heard them before.
That's what I listen to—new music.
If it is not new, it must not be very good.
I only like new movies and new books.
It must be new or I won't like it.
Old SUCKS!
New is today and I live for the day, motherfucker!
History is BULLSHIT.
I make history.
I AM THE NEW!
Now, if you'll excuse me, I am going to skateboard in
OUTER SPACE!

THIS POEM IS ORANGE

That means it is on HIGH ALERT
You should read this poem with a heightened sense of
    caution
It is subversive and should be viewed as a threat
I wrote it with a pen full of anthrax
If you are touching it you should take some Cipro
I have already taken some Cipro so that when I read it
    out loud
It is not so toxic—or is it?

It is your duty to report this poem to John Ashcroft.
Laura Bush would not let me read this poem in the
    rose garden

THIS LINE HAS A SPECIAL CODED MESSAGE
    FOR OSAMA BIN LADEN

Did you get the message? If so, please turn me in to
    Homeland Security

This is why you'll never see this poem on Def Poetry on
    HBO.
It is also why they cancelled "Sex in the City" because
    Kim Catrall's
Areolas contained secret messages to the Taliban
Bill Clinton and Bob Dole will debate this poem next
    week on 60 minutes
This poem will not comply with George and Colin's
    demands

I will not disarm this poem!
It is a time bomb ready to explode in the face of
    political hypocrisy and bullshit
WAR MONGERING!

I will continue to manufacture more poems like this
    one until the President that
NOBODY VOTED FOR ends this war that NOBODY
    ASKED FOR!!!!!

How about a nice game of chess?

OF SHAPPYLAND I SING

I'm not sure where I live anymore
I used to think I lived in America
America—where I have the freedom to say what I like
    and do what I like
Where my vote counts
Not for the American President
But for the American Idol
America hates Frenchy, no?
Would you like freedom fries with that?
Just don't wear a t-shirt with a peace symbol on it at
    your local mall
But feel free to keep shopping so bombs can keep
    dropping!

I'll tell you what, Georgie boy, I'll give you your $300
    back if you'll
BACK THE FUCK UP
And admit that you are a fake president
    (BOOOOOOOOOOO!)
Fighting a fake war (BOOOOOOOOOOOO!)
Yeah, BOOOOOOOO!
That's MOORE like it!
How dare he make a movie about this country being
    violent and gun-crazy
And win an Oscar and speak out against a BULLSHIT
    war? BOOOOOOO!
Yeah, cuz, dude, 9/11 was like a movie
And this war is like a video game, dude!

Well, fucking game over!
Because no Springsteen song is gonna make me feel
    better

And I don't need Peter, Dan and Tom giving me
    updates and their opinion
On how it's going every half hour!

What I do need is a map, because I don't know where
    I'm standing these days.
What is this "America" you speak of?

I live in a land of candy and snack cakes and there's a
    Toys R Us the size of a football stadium.
Where I can buy ice cream from a musical truck and
    watch puppies sniff each
Other's butts in the dog park.
Where girls smell nice and children build spaceships
    out of Legos.
Where the beer is always flowing and anyone can jump
    on stage and spout
Crazy poetry or sing "Suspicious Minds."
Where me and my girlfriend call each other "Snoo" and
    dream of owning a
Wiener dog together because we're retarded in love
    like that.
That's where I live.
And I'm sure a lot of you live in your own little worlds
    as well, but
I'm willing to bet that none of them are like what the
    government calls
"America."
It's time for our worlds to collide
And create the party planet we deserve and not the
Nightmare world we live in today.

WORST POLITICAL POEM EVER!

Don't get me started, you . . you . . . you
Don't fuck with me, Mister Man!
I'll send a team of inspectors to search your asshole for
      hidden bombs.
I am a madman!
I am the great Satan!
I am willing to spend millions and millions of other
      people's hard earned
Dollars just to talk shit about you on national television!
You are a silly person!
Don't make me taunt you a second time!
I'm super serious, you guys!
It's my football and I'll pull it away from you when you
      come running up to
Kick it one time, Baby Pop!
I'm gonna get two ice cream cones.
One with two scoops and sprinkles for me and one
      plain vanilla cone for you
And when you reach out for yours I'll "accidentally"
      drop yours in the sand.
You dropped your ice cream!
You dropped your ice cream!
And you can't have none cuz you can't afford it!
But I can, MUTHAFUCKA!
I can buy and sell your ass like little green houses and
      little red hotels
It's a monopoly—OF FEAR!
I'm close personal friends of the Parker Brothers.
We were in the Skull and Crossbones Quilting Bee so
      buzz off!
America's BIG—yeah, yeah, yeah!
It's not small—no, no, no!

It's wabbit season
Duck season
Wabbit season
Duck and cover
Cuz I'm waxing and milking all of my dirty bombs!
Begun this clone war has!
I intendo to finish what my daddy started
I'm blaming you for the stink
Even if we're the ones who farted!

BUTTERFLY

Where ya flyin' to, lil' butterfly?
Where ya flyin' to?
Is there some big butterfly ball to go to?
A lovely party in the sky, butterfly?
Did you bring a dish to share?
Did you?
Some cream of mushroom soup with green beans
and Baco-bits to share?
That pyrex dish is mighty heavy.
How'd you get it up there?!?
You're flyin' pretty,
flyin' pretty high.
Did ya need a couple drinks?
A couple drinks to get you by?
And FLY, BUTTERFLY?!?
Your mother's worried sick,
worried about your crazy drinkin' butterfly ways.
You've seen better days butterfly,
you've seen better days.
Remember those days on the road with the Doobie
        Brothers
settin' up the mic stands and gettin' high?
I mean, REALLY FUCKING HIGH, BUTTERFLY?
Jesus was just all right by you, butterfly!
And then those bastard Doobies (some of them weren't
        even brothers, man!),
They stranded you in Pittsburgh
and they made you cry
like a Native American
standing on the freeway
where some litter has been carelessly thrown.
Now you just flutter-flutter-flutter on by.

Flutter-flutter-flutter
away from your problems.
You're quite the lucky fellow.
Butterfly?
Yes, Shappy?
I want to kill you.
Butterfly?
Yes, Shappy?
I wanna . . . I wanna . . .
flutter-flutter-flutter

I AM THAT NERD

I am that Nerd
I am the Eternal Nerd of Spoken Word
I am that Nerd
What can I say
I spent all my rent money
buying action figures on ebay
but I didn't come here to chit-chat
I came here to role-play
I will smite thee with my 12-sided die
you better watch out cuz I'm coming at you
with my nerd eye!
I'm rocking you like Geddy Lee
I would talk to more girls if they didn't make me
want to pee myself
I'm a magical elf
you better keep your hands off my Star Wars shelf!
That's right bee-yatch
that's a mint in package Jawa
with it's original plastic cape

don't that flip your switch?
just like the switch that Han Solo hit
on Boba Fett
that caused him to fall into the Sarlacc Pit

Lest we forget?
I'm coming at you in 3-D
I'm keeping it reel with 2 ee's y'see?
for I am the master of all that I view
for I'm so much smarter and nerdier than you!
I had Stephen Hawking gawking and gasping for air
blew his mind with my knowledge
and he fell straight out his chair
I beat Matthew Broderick at War Games with my Atari
I dug up Einstein's bones and made them say
I'm sorry for that weak ass theory of relativity
cuz MC^2 = me, see?
I'm the plastic baby Jesus in your mind's nativity
I'll deprogram your mind with my Commodore 64
I'm so rich in nerd power
I make Bill Gates feel poor!
I will kidnap George Lucas from Skywalker Ranch
and lock him in my basement
until he removes Jar Jar Binks
from every frame of Phantom Menace
and Attack of the Clones
and replaces him with me
For I am an ancient Jedi knight
only Yoda be older
I knocked Mork's space egg out of orbit
and made it crash in Boulder
I liquified Alf and ET and drank of their plasma
I'm the muthafucka wot gave Darth Vader asthma!
For only I can unravel the mystery of the Sith

cuz I just knocked over the black monolith
with my boner!
Bet you didn't see that one coming!
I'm a mystical nerd shaman who never stops drumming
on your stupid stupid minds
for I am the original cast of Star Trek
and you are Deep Space Nine!

Sha-Clock Spock
Ommmmmmmmm

I HATE YUPPIES POEM #138

All right you young, upwardly mobile FUCKS!
You win! I give up, okay?
Just power walk and roller blade
over my bruised and bleeding slacker ASS!
Kick me and my freaky friends
out of loft spaces and cheap apartments
and go condo, PUSSYCAT, BUILD! BUILD!
Kick all the old me out of my favorite dive bars
charge me a cover
and get me a $22 chocolate martini while
you're at it, JACK!
Keep crowding up all the bars on the weekends
with your cell phones and cigar smoke
(but not in New York, nyah, nyah)
and frat brothers and sorority sisters
and your incessant yak-yak-yakkity-yak-yak
about everything and nothing.
Put an ATM on every corner
and never throw the bums a dime in your prime

and how many roads must a man walk down
before he can find himself a STARBUCKS?!?!
The answer, my friend, is TWO BLOCKS!
How is your coffee, sir?
Too Black? Too Strong?
TOO BLACK? TOO STRONG?
Well, you better start tearing down those
        housing projects
so you can park your URBAN ROAD VEHICLE
in a secure urban environment!
Continue not to support any local band, artist
        or poet,
feel free to talk loudly over anyone trying to
entertain you with anything that might
cause you to think more than you would
watching an episode of WILL & GRACE!
Keep "improving" our fair city
Whitewash all of our city's dirty, grimy heritage
into a Martha Stewart merry-go-round of
MEDIOCRITY!
ME?
I'm getting off this crazy thing, Dick.

STINKY

Boy howdy! I am one smelly muthafucka!
Let's face it—I stink!
I don't "smell right"
I smell really wrong
horribly wrong
My friends no longer tell me
to take a shower

they tell me to see a doctor
because they are convinced that no
human being
could possibly be so odorific
so incredibly officious to the olfactory
flowers will wilt when I pass
and puppies fall over and die
as they sniff my fragrant ass.
When I take off my socks
scientists flock to my house and seal it off
like that scene in "E.T."
because there is something alien about that stench
        coming from me.
Imagine, if you will, a sweaty jock strap
floating in a rusty bucket of cat urine
sitting next to a block of
month-old government cheese
that has been sprayed with Lysol
and left sitting in the hot summer sun
then maybe you'll understand
why I am called "The Stinky One."
Every fart—a work of art.
A glorious symphony of sound,
a composition of chili cheese fries,
cheap beer, cabbage and broccoli.
So when I lay down my butt trumpet solo
you'll want to keep your distance, see?
But of all the stinky players
in this game of life,
I'm not the worst one on the bench.
'Cuz there's a lot of stinky suckers in this world
who leave a fouler stench:
people who don't tip—stink
politicians—stink

right-to-lifers who bomb clinics—stink
people who collect beanie babies—stink
critics—stink
lawyers—stink
deadbeat dads—stink
child molesters—stink
garth brooks—stinks
alternative rock—stinks
guys with short hair on top
and long hair in the back—stink
guys who write poems like this—stink stink stink
to the highest heavens!
And what about yuppies, Shappy?
What about those goddamn urban vehicle drivin'
hummus gobblin' mail order catalog orderin'
condo dwellin' the whole world
my fuckin' oyster shuckin' YUPPIES!!!
Well, they may smell good to the real estate developers
and personal trainers and the producers
of *Friends* and *Ally McBeal*
but no amount of designer fragrance
from Calvin Klein will ever mask the heinous stench
of self-satisfied bullshit
from ME
The Stinkiest Motherfucker On Earth!

BISEXUAL ADOLESCENT ESKIMO

I feel the cold wind in my bones.
It is as chilling as the first time you took me
to the back of you igloo
. . .and touched me
underneath my pelt.
Those long winter days and nights,
no sunshine
only the light in your eyes
keeps me warm.
Oh, to be a bisexual, adolescent Eskimo.
I chew on my pain like so much blubber
for my emotional pipeline is cracked.
And my feet?
My bisexual adolescent eskimo feet
are always . . . cold

WHAT'S THAT IN YOUR HANDS?

what's that in your hands, love?
what's that . . . in your hands?
why, it's my nutsack, isn't it?
my tender, little, fuzzy nutsack
careful, my love!
treat it gently and gingerly
for it's quite sensitive and precious
teasing tickle—fine
playful pinch—fine
but please, love,
don't punch him
don't kick him

don't pull on him as if he were
the starting cord of a lawn mower
I guess what I'm getting at is. . .
kiss him?
won't you please lick my nutsack?
lick it with Riunite on ice
lick it like a luscious lolly
lick it with vim and vigor, by golly
lick it like a delicious "iced cream"
lick it after a shot of Jim Beam
lick it like you just don't care
(and please don't choke on a tiny black hair!)
keep licking my beanbag,
I'm begging you please
lick it—I swear there will be no headcheese
with a q-tip I will wipe it clean
SO KEEP ON LICKIN', YOU CRAZY KID!
lick my nutsack—
you'll be glad you did!

HAIKU

loving you is hard
but not as hard as Dokken
that shit truly rocks

A LOVELY LOVE POEM FOR OO!

Hello, my friend!
Do you remember me?
It's your old pal—Love!
Remember how we used to hang out
and make each other laugh?
We'd titter like the small children running though the
sprinkler on a warm summer's day!
"Tee-hee!" we'd laugh. "Tee-hee!"
Then I would punch you in the face, screaming;
"I LOVE YOU!"
And when you wouldn't say "I love you" back
I would kick you in your private area
crying, "No, seriously, I really fucking love you,
goddammit!"
Oh, those were wonderful, innocent times.
It was almost as tender as the episode
of Beverly Hills 90210 when Donna lost
her virginity to Brian Austin Green.
Welcome aboard—it's Love.
Oh, I'm sorry, did I catch you at a bad time?
I'm sorry, I'll come back later, when you are
ready for me.
Okay—good-bye—then
Knock-knock
Who's there?
Allo again, it's me, Love!
You can't get rid of me!
Because I love you so fucking much, baby!
You can shun me
you can kick me to the curb
as they say on Rikki Lake.
You can send me back to the kitchen like a
piece of undercooked meat

but I will come back juicier
and even more tender and delicious.
You will savor the flavor of love.
You will choke on the gristle of my love.
You will accidentally bite down
on the fork of my passion and hurt your teeth!
The same teeth that smile at me when I come
strolling down the hallway of your heart!
　　　Look out!
Because love comes sliding down the hill
really super fast like Chevy Chase in
Christmas Vacation!
Or sometimes it is really slow like watching
every episode of *Twin Peaks* in a row
because like the midget in that show
　　　Life is short.
So short in fact that sometimes you
walk right past it on your way to
Starbucks where a young person in
a baseball cap will yell out your
order for all to hear:
Let me get a grande foamy feeling
　　　for you!
And sprinkle it with all the cinnamon
　　　of lust!
I will dribble down your chin,
　　　lover!
Let me dab that for you!
　　　Dab dab dab!
Just call Dabney Coleman
　　　9 to 5—
What a way to make a loving!
Cuz I'm a-loving you lover!
Whether you want me to or not!

Moonshine Shorey

Moonshine was born in the woods of Vermont and spent most of his early years having to deal with the cold. The youngest of four, Moonshine took time to be a dancer and traveled the East Coast, Russia, Costa Rica and Newfoundland. When he hung up his ballet shoes he decided to spend his time hating high school and started running the roads. Along with going to school to be a nurse's aide, becoming a track and field thrower and a general misfit, Moonshine started writing poetry on the side.

After an ill-fated move to the South to be a print model and recreation director, Moonshine returned to Vermont to befriend deadbeat dads, single moms and wayward teens. After a few years as a Lot Lizard at the Exit 2 Truck Stop he moved to New York City to do relief work for September 11th. He grew dissatisfied while running a children's literary program in a language he didn't speak.

After a stint at the Nuyorican's open mic, a friend brought him to a new poetry club. From that point he knew his home would be the Bowery Poetry Club, and informed Bob Holman, the proprietor of the BPC, that he would work two weeks for free, then Bob could pay him or Moonshine would just leave. Bob started paying him that day. Henceforth, Moonshine, "Moony," has slung drinks, poetry, and love from the bar at the BPC.

While a bartender/artist-in-residence at the BPC, Moonshine has also become a downtown art star, winning the 2005 Mr. Lower East Side Pageant. He is also a provocative burlesque performer, an award-winning bartender, and host of the very successful Closed Mic!, "Midnights with Moonshine" every Wednesday.

Moonshine would like to thank, in no particular order: God; beer; good looks; Mom and the rest of the family; Anna and the truck stop crew; R.I.P; Deb Hadaka,the best supporter of a wayward teen; luckydave, for your everlasting support; Bob Holman; lesbos; Diane O'Debra and the rest of the Art Star community for accepting me with open arms and thighs; cheeseburgers; Jennifer Blowdryer, my colleague in life; the ever-changing BPC staff; Ben McCarthy, a good lesson learned; drunks; loose women and tight men; and all the people who have put up with my shit over the years—just think of all the shit to come when I finally "make it!"

22A

Autumn sautés the trees with tangerine
Along the two-dimensional cardboard mountain-side
The mountain adores the creek
It always walks so softly past its feet
Never following the highway's hazardous ways

A Letter to a Little Girl

Dear Whom It May Concern:

In this world of making mistakes to learn, I
thought I'd save you thirty years and tell you
what the world really fears.

You must be a good little girl and wear your
pink little bows and over-sized glasses, so
when you hit acne and puberty you won't fall
through the cracks and lose yourself to the
first man or boy to put out his hand. You must
learn to be a woman in a nicely wrapped forty-
minute health class, or from two people who
won't listen to each other, much less you. You
must also give the best years of your life (or
at least the best years of your thighs) to
your prom date or mate who says he loves you.
He loves the blue in your eye, especially when
you cry. If he raises his hand it had better
be to ask if he can open the door, sweep the
floor, take out the trash or kiss your ass.
Because if you stand by your man, the dominos
will take effect and rectify the situation.
All your relationships with men should not
bend under six inches of flaccid skin. Don't
hide in that doll house thinking all you need
is a perfect spouse, a cat named Fluffy, a dog
named Spot. Don't get caught up in that
fairytale or dream because it is not at all

what you think. Cinderella spent the last ten
years pulling broken glass out of her feet,
scrubbing cum stains out of satin sheets.
Little Miss Muffet ran away with Little Bo
Peep. To hell with tending sheep, woman's work
is not finding some jerk and polishing his
knob, that is not at all the job. Don't long
to be that princess for her dress is always
covered with stains, and what will you wear
girl when it rains down like the tiers on your
wedding cake, leaving you nothing but another
orgasm to fake. Please do not be scared of the
Big Bad Wolf. His bark is worse than his bite
and a fight. Red Riding Hood might do that dog
some good. Teach him how to sit, stay and beg
for taking the last thousand years and using
your fears against you. Because who does he
think he is, pissing standing up is not
enough. You need to sway your hips and send
him in a tail-spin. You need to grin showing
him you can win this world and rule this land
without holding his hand. I believe there
still needs to be prosecution for this
institution where they put you in second place
not for silver but for slivers put between
your legs. So ladies take your eggs and
runaway runaway run run runaway to No Man's
Land. No longer will there be any over easy,
sunny side or fried and scrambled messages of
what a girl should be, take at least this
little bit from me. So Little Girl if you've
been totally burdened by what I've said, brush
your teeth and go back to bed.

                    Love,
                    Moonshine

A Note To The World Trade Center

I know how it feels,
I was the biggest kid in my class too.

Stone's Purpose

> *A stone's only purpose in life*
> *is to make it off the mountain*
> *into the sea.*

That was the only lesson Bear and I learned in our
Vermont Ecology class our senior year of high school. We
were too busy skipping class. We drove the back roads of
Benson, hitting joints and swilling Labatt Blue. Hoping
no one knew we had left school. We never did get
caught.

Bear and I met in the spring of '89. Too young to care
about orientations and girl relations. Our only motivation
was to kill that big ass frog that lay in Lake Bebe. We
tried like hell skipping slate off the surface, but he never
did get caught, that frog. But now at the age of 18

> *We were dying to run the roads*
> *Too old to be killing toads.*
> *Heard the wind's whispers...*
> *never turn back never turn back*

On graduation night, both of us were completely
shocked as our diplomas were handed to us without our
having to give an excuse where we'd been. I swore I had
failed Geometry, and you knew you had failed Gym. But
just the same, when would I need to know how to do a
proof and you'd know the dimensions of a pickle ball

court. We said goodbye over a poorly rolled blunt and a couple shots of vodka. The next day I moved to Georgia, you to a shanty shack in the woods that you had built yourself.

We were dying to run those roads.
Too old to be catching colds. We
held our breath. And trusted our hearts
would work out the rest

A year later after I had found myself lost in the Mecca of teen angst I left the peaches and went back to the apples. You were the first person I saw, holding a Long Trail Ale in one hand and trying to catch your aspiration in the other. I knew with both of us, that our dreams were right at our finger tips, but we just couldn't get a good enough grip. We decided from that day forth we could count on the other for five finger discounts of pale ale and dope whenever the other needed.

We were dying to run those roads.
Too young to be fitting molds.
Catching our breath with fishing nets
but never throwing anything back.

We saw each other here and there and time to time as years passed. Always picking up where we last left off, You want to burn one? You were the one to throw me my going away party when I moved to New York City. Making sure you stayed awake long enough to finish the last game of Asshole, last can of beer, last line of Vicodin.

We were dying to run those roads.
Too young to be doing what we're told
Hoping the other would never forget how
to get home.

So, when I read the newspaper the day after you died, I knew there had to be more than one mistake. "Benson Man Dies in Car Wreck" was the headline. You were Bear — not a man or boy, just a guy that I was promised would always be around. You couldn't have flipped your car leaving the bar going to Castleton. Black ice was the cause, the article said. The paper too proud to embarrass your family. But they kept calling you Andrew, every time they addressed you they called you Andrew. I knew you as Bear, and now I was to leave the city to go and look at this man named Andrew and say my goodbyes.

You died on these roads.
Too young and old
to be lost in the fold.
You must sleep and I must go.

Keep from getting caught crying at your grave as I move my finger tips over the name (Bear) in parentheses on your tombstone. Wondering what went wrong as they play some song about how much we will miss you. Where do I fit in the scale of worth? I, your stoner friend, who tried to be there 'til the end. If you had just told me that friends die and not just people, could I or you have done something different? Different with our lives? The only thing for certain is, you never did make it to the sea. But as the salt water falls from my face onto the cold stone of your permanent marker, I like to think you did. At least in my eyes.

A Tall Glass of Water

I swallow
Trees shake
Tea turns cold
I let the day out at noon
Six has come too soon
Leaves fall
Legs lock tight
I spit

Bi Passing

For the girls:
Boy, have we come so far
oh so far,
It is too bad physics won't let us
make more of this
now please stop waiting

For the boys:
I like dick
Thank god for me
I've got my own

Cacti

Emerald ovals that belong only under an Amarillo
    skyline.
Colored daggers spear through gems
Caution signs for accidents that will never occur.
Built from the sand up
They stretch lifeless limbs
A paraplegic without a crutch or cane.
Not interested in the swaying ways of cousins and
    friends.
Content to be seen as the camel of the Southwest.
Water, so overrated it states as it falls into coyote sleep.

Driftwood

The living dead
standing in their cemetery
with their hands stretched out
holding the sky from falling
It has no legs
they whisper
hoping the horizon doesn't hear
come to our cemetery
learn to stand still
they request of me
no no I say
I am more kin to the ocean
the pain of being a shade of water

Epiphany

"You're a bitch!"

In the nicest way
Possible I place
This epiphany
On the mantle
Next to the fact
That I, like Jesus,
Was a bastard child

Love is a black
And white film
That will never
Leave your teeth
And the realization
That we all get
When we turn nineteen

That our parents
Are people too
They choked on
Their first cigarette
Can't do long division
And felt dirty after their
First one-night stand

Eulogy in Me Flat

everyone was doing it &
you thought once would be fine &
it was alright &
you tried it again &
boy, did it take the edge off &
why hadn't you started sooner &
it's only for fun &
it'll be our little secret &
you start doing it more &
nobody really notices &
you're fine

YOU STOP

asking if it's changing you &
a little before work won't make a difference &
a little at work won't count & a little after work
won't matter & a little becomes a lot &
who cares because you can finally feel your heart &
people start to notice &
people start to talk &
it's none of their business &
they're only jealous of you &

YOU STOP

talking to them &
you make new friends &
they do it with you all the time &
it still feels so good &
they show you how to use your looks &
charm & money &

it all starts to become a dust storm slowly &
you find yourself going out more &
drinking more &
smoking more &
on your knees more &
snorting more &
saluting more cocks more &
then

YOU STOP

being able to sleep regularly &
you blame it on his smell &
your nerves &
the nerve &
days pass &
weeks &
months &

you wonder what happened to your friends &
it all becomes familiar &
these bars are all the same &
these bars are all the same &
you're frustrated with everyone &
even in yourself &
you keep going down the same old Dead End St. &
now penthouses don't seem high enough &
where is all my time going &
where is all MY time going &
where is last week's paycheck &
where is the rent &
where is all MY TIME going &
where do you live again &
WHERE is all MY TIME going &

where do I live again &
where am I going &
WHERE is ALL MY TIME going &
who cares becomes a question &
one day you find yourself again &

YOU STOP

&
ask GOD what has happened
&
you don't hear back
&
you never hear back

Exit 2

> *"Of course my work is nothing,*
> *compared to those who work on trucks."*
> —Taylor Mead

The beer is flat
Like the preteen girls
Who sip it while showing off
K-Mart pearls to men who cannot remember
Their kid's middle name on a good day
But just the same

This is Anna and I and we are
Lot lizards at Exit 2 24-hour Truck Stop
And this is all a part of the bargain, slurping
Free cappuccinos from push-button machines

Downing Slim Jims with ease and having
Trucker men call us Honey, Baby, Sugar
Anything but late for dinner. And of course we would
    call them
Fuck Face, Pig Fucking Sons a Bitches
But never to their face.
Now and then a pet name would slip
And they would think we were just being bitches
Which was fine with us, Anna and I
Were tougher than a two day-old diner hotdog,
Harder than reheated chili.
We were known to stalk that lot at three A.M.,
Bitch knives under our tongues, hearts
On our sleeves with Cheshire smiles on cold-ass faces.

My first trucker was named Robert Redstar.
I never knew his god-given name,
Just took what his buddies called him
And put it to who he hauled for.
He was nothing special, but he would throw me
Joints and 40's on occasion.
I knew I reminded him of the nephew he never got the
    chance
To molest but he never touched me never touched me,
Content to have a voice with some warmth other than
The over-heated engine. Anna fell head

Over heels for the nastiest fucker
Named Jamie Kraft. I knew he was crazy
When I snuck into his cab late at night to steal
Some Camels and noticed twenty open pine tree-
Shaped cherry air fresheners. He would disappear
For weeks on end and not tell Anna where he was,
Until she filled his voice mailbox with threats to his:

Cats, kids, wife, him and then finally to herself.
Then he would show up, knowing a 19-year-old white
    trash girl
With a Whip-it addiction probably didn't have that
    much to lose.

Anna and I would spend our time at the truck stop
Eating Ben & Jerry's in the heated handicapped
    bathroom,
Reading the Rutland *Herald* 20 times a day, picking
On flatlanders and talking to truckers.
Our talks would be,
You should have been there when I lost those cops
In the swamp, little did they know I had a half
An ounce in my crotch, and I would say,
You should have been there when I did
Those three tabs of acid and had to go to the hospital
To work. But on those cold dark nights when the
    freezing
Rain was so much like men who cannot decide if they
    want
To stay put or disappear down the gutter, the talks
    would be
You should have been there, for me when he drove by
At midnight and didn't stop or even pull his Jake brake
To say hello. And I would say, *You should have been
    there,*
For me, when I met his wife.
Wives were inevitable, like
An appendix. You knew most people had them, but you
    weren't
Sure why. But we believed them, those truckers, when
They promised us the world knowing the only stake
They claimed was to the cot in the back of their cab.

I did move away from Exit 2
Passed the triple-stacked cheeseburgers
With mayo, A1 and Tabasco
Passed those shit-faced weekends
Speeding tickets on dirt roads
Passed all of it
I look back at Exit 2
Much like a car accident
Where the car is totaled
But everyone gets out alright
To tell their story the next day
At the pumps. No matter how far
I feel from Exit 2 today
Nothing turns me on more
Than the smell of diesel on Carhartts.

Fairy's Tale

FAGGOT! QUEER!
FUDGE PACKIN' FAIRY! AC/DC!
LIGHT IN THE LOAFERS!
ASS PIRATE! SISSY BOY!
HERSHEY HIGHWAY HITCHIKIN' HOMO!

(this is for you)

I always felt that my gayness was something
I had to wait to acquire,
Like my first beer or driver's license.

No sense in coming out at the age of five,
When they'll tell you it's only a stage. When
You are in your cage, they'll pay admission
To keep their suspicions. Scars

Behind bars. But step outside —
Open season on your hide.

I've been on my knees but not for praying
Listening to what the priest been saying

Hell is Home for Homos

You take the D away from devil you got evil
You take the E away from evil you got vile
You take the V away from vile you got ill
You take the I away from ill you got

LLLLLLLLLLLLLLLLLLLLLL
LLLLLLLLLLLLLLLLLLLLLLLLLLLLLLLLLLLL
LLLLLLLLLLLLLLL

Which is where those homosexuals be!

In HELL!

But those preachers been teachers
To many an altar boy. Showing them the "Hand of God"
Seems to be partial to taking down Fruit of the Looms
        But who am I to blame when every sexual
        perversion
Is placed on my shoulders these pebbles become
    boulders
And I'm no Atlas, but at last I want the space to erase the
Misconceptions of all these men's perceptions of me

FIRST

To the man who said he was just testing the waters
He needed to experiment
Well I meant to tell you I'm no scientist but your
    hypothesis
Has got a flaw, from what I saw you had no problem
Getting on the floor on all fours

SECOND

To those men who say they're straight by fate,
In the locker room do not assume I'm checking out
    your dick.
Because this squirrel needs more than just some nuts
    and a stick
The sequoia between my knees needs more than just a
    quick breeze, soil and
Son if you come thinking you are the one
And knowing what ought to be

Number   THREE

We had better have more than sodomy in common
Don't throw me your bone to chew on like a rawhide
    toy
Cause that ain't it, the question isn't if I swallow or
    spit

SHIT

I grew up on the fag farm
I woke to the cry of the morning cock
Wanting me to get up, but not off and I
Negate the mistake that I need to be
Plowed or hoed or shown the back road
To paradise.

Because to you that might sound nice,
But I have gotten there just by playing solitaire

And   I'm the 10% tax that you won't pay gratuity
Because I lack your systematic sexual continuity.
I am queerer than a three dollar bill, but I will not be
    the one to pay
For my past wrecks, past pecs, past sex

And no longer will you be the one to deposit your sums
    inside my
Buns, no more quick withdrawals because I will
    PUNCH not
Bitch slap your ass
Because truth be told
My thighs sigh when they see you cumming.

I'm not running to get on any pride parade
But if I decide to ride just because I'm there doesn't
    mean I'm
Wearing a brassiere   and no
I will not disappear or calm down or change my FONT
    and Fuck you I'm not moving to
           VERMONT   Because I
will find my end of
the rainbow no matter
If I have to scratch scream or pillage
And I'm not finding it in Chelsea or the Village because
I'm standing UP
    Standing OUT   and I'm standing
        ALONE

First Date/Break Up

You held your body against me.
Nothing is better than that.

You held your body against me.
Nothing, is better than that.

The flowers finally went to bed, and died in their sleep

He treated my mouth like a womb
It seemed easier,
to align my teeth, subordinate soldiers
Ready for our war
The timeline of my tongue can not account
for every native's death or birth of screaming kids
the buckets made for water now hold skin
call it mine, or bomb
it will be simple detonation for
death will never be a proper noun

Poem for all the lives I lived without me

Someone is calculating the clouds
        Today
Amen stiffens a softened black
Hanging over the half-hearted
The drawbacks of living
        Stay true
Like fingerprints, murky
Fog that battles the smallest lighthouse

For the asshole who said I could never put it to words

There is a jar that I keep inside my chest
that holds all your kisses and saliva

BUT THIS AIN'T NO LOVE POEM

It's not meant to scratch that itch
or flick your switch

cause I'm pushing the buttons now   BITCH

You are as authentic as a burrito from Taco Bell.
I'm doing swell.
Is that what you want to hear?
Coming up to me after three short months
wondering how I've been. Like dodge ball
is to ducking and Cinemax is to fucking.
You weren't lucking out
when you asked me how I am. But my mother
told me never to talk when my mouth is full of
COCKSUCKER MOTHERFUCKER, I'M GOING
TO FUCK YOU UP WITH MY FUCK STICK YOU
FUCKFACE MOTHERFUCKER!!!!

Spins inside my head. But all I can say is I miss you
       hold me.
I say everything wrong, but I would have been your
       virgin bride
             the secret you hide
I should have been your bread crumb trail
             the wind in your sail
I should have been the sea you swim
             anything but HIM

You found yourself in him like I found myself in you
on a nightly basis, running your bases like Mark McGwire
      homeruns were inevitable
and you were incredible . . . . . . maybe
    like the Hulk,
        green to my ways

The butterfly vacated the cocoon
too soon
A purposeful metamorphosis for . . .

So, when you told me you were leaving me for someone
    else

I totally understood what you meant

I just wanted to tell you

I was giving you up

for Lent.

Get over it (yourself)

Crying is the only thing
In life
Guaranteed to give
You tears

Don't say I never gave you anything

Half Lies

(white trash gossip)

She must have an awesome crotch or a whole lot of money to keep that man. Did you hear? They're giv'in their kids to the state, since his skank-ass wife jumped ship and moved to West Virginia with that jigaboo who sold opium out of his Camaro down by the Piggly Wiggly. Which wasn't that big of a suprise, see'in they really hadn't been together since Buck was born with that touch of retardation. He blamed it on her for drinking that bottle of Boone's Farm and chasing it with Xanax when she was four months knocked up. He had always wondered why they hadn't left him in the hospital from the get go. Their eldest, Kimber, when she fell out of that sloppy hole her mother called a pussy she started screaming. When she stopped doing that, she started pissing the bed. She didn't stop doing that until that ugly-ass trucker cold-cocked her in the face when she ruined his WWF vintage sheets. She wet them down right to the mattress. That was about the time she started fucking everything in sight: the Mexican milkman, her dad's mechanic, the dyke bus-driver. All this wouldn't have been that big of a deal if she had kept her hands off the bitch's son. Uh huh, that's what sold her up shit creek without a paddle. She was too young to be acting like a two-bit tranny hooker looking for a hot beef injection. Him old enough to know even finger bang'in that little ho would send him to the big house. But the bitch hav'in the money from opening up two H&R Blocks and a rumored awesome crotch nothing was happening to her son. No siree. So, that would have been it, her and her brother going to the State, if Berta hadn't run her mouth to Chet. Chet who had gotten blowjobs from the little slut in the dugout behind the grade school. So he had some loyalty to the little bitch. So when she found out, you know what she did? She stole three hundred dollars from the bitch's purse, keyed the bitch's car and hitchhiked to the Greyhound station. Then headed to Florida, just like all stray cats and men lookin' to do construction.

On My Way To Work

The babies in their carriages are all kinds of happy
Wa wa da da ma ma goo goo
Don't throw me out with the bath water

The family in front of the funeral home are all kinds of
        sad
Wa wa da da ma ma goo goo
Don't plant me in a grave

The teens in back of the bus are all kinds of happy
Bang bang la la Bang Bang la la
Yes you can hold me

The parents in their home are all kinds of sad
Bang bang la la Bang Bang la la
Yes you can hold me down

All of this makes me think fire was bad from the
        beginning

How Does the Knife Pronounce Love?

In the third person, or by sight
GOD
I want you to tell me your last name
Then take my laughs and your legs
and go to wherever
you make next

Pecking Order Etiquette

Why do we call her Rose
When Dandelion be her name
Do you suppose
They could be the same?

Icicles

Frozen phallic symbols
Commune onto my roof
Giving birth to missiles
Sending them to the Earth
Firmly being planted
To grow until the thaw
Then giving birth one by one
Leaving winter raw

Slot machines & Sodomy

Like Las Vegas
I will look different by morning

Match

When I met you
People said I had met my match
But you fail to light me up
Or even go with black

New Math

654646696856767654644 NONE OF YOUR
98779979999 CRYPTOMATIC 313131333131
MATHEMATIC 32117533234733322555113
159753224562 LOVE 4209885 WILL EVER 97
+ 4698 ADD 5842254463014472119712300055
0000000000 UP 00000000000000000000

Quadzilla's Revenge

Fuck you, Richard Simmons!
Go to hell, Stairmaster!
My hour glass figure is done going through Daylight
      Savings!

All the temptations and cravings you throw in my
      face
Make me ill, or pop a pill or throw up dinner just to be
      thinner

I'm tired of running the race to see if I take up too
    much space or if my
Face looks like some drugged up anorexic model we
    see on every
Healthy Living magazine
I've seen those fads come and go just like my rolls on
    the Diet of No
Carbos, No Ho Ho's, No Fast Food, No Real Food, No
    Salt, No Sugar, No Snacks,
No Meals!!
    Soouuuwwwwwwwweeeeeeeeeeeeeeeeeeeeeeeee
Makes me squeal like the pig I must be

Having everyone ask, Hun, want that last piece of cake?
Dressing in Husky, having people guessing
I must be big-boned or retain water
    BITCH, I RETAIN PIZZA

My nerves were spent on a gym membership I never
    went more than once
To have those would-be "models" point at my keg and
    tell me
That's where a six pack should be. Well, let them have
    their muscles and Brussels sprouts, beans and
    lettuce. Let me super size my thighs with pies   Let
    me enlarge my belly with jars of jelly   Let me fill
    my hips with chips and dip and when I'm ready
To make a magical reversal, I'll just tune in to an

INFOMERCIAL

DO YOU LONG TO BE SKINNY?
Do you want to look like Brad Pitt or Julia Roberts?
Well, just be our lab rat and say good bye to fat
IS BEING OVERWEIGHT KEEPING YOU
FROM THE LOVE OF YOUR LIFE?

Well, sacrifice that broken heart
A heart attack is just the start
Pay us in a lifetime of easy payments of
    low self esteem and pain and
In no time at all   You'll stay the same

We put the DIE in DIET
So don't miss your chance to get your kit
Call 1-800 CROCK OF SHIT
and soon enough you'll fit into that size
5 - 4 - 3 - 2 - 1 lift off into the atmosphere
Because in a size 0 you'll just disappear

So Heather Locklear, Tom Cruise, Calista Flockhart,
    Gwyneth Paltrow and the rest of the anorexic
    agenda it is time to change
We're getting on my bootylicious train and going to Sizzler
And we're gonna hit that buffet line again again again
    again again again again again again again. . . . . .

So little girl scout I will buy a box of cookies as a matter
    of fact
Just make sure they're
    LOW FAT

Separation

I learned that Vietnam calls Nam the American War
In a Women's History class
I learned about women in a Men's Room
I learned about men while on my knees
I learned about knees from scrapes and cuts
I learned about cuts from steak knives
Which were made in Vietnam

Straight Men & Subways

Since I moved to NYC
I seem to be spending
A good deal
Of time wanting and waiting
For them   to

<.come.>

Seventh Street Sestina

Part I

Pale skin bathes in artificial light.
The rays trace her steps back,
To when she walked the halls of high
School. She wore her Catholic dress,
And dreamt the dreams of the Supreme Angel,
The angel would teach her about true love.

She knew so much about true love.
Oh yes, with every passing car light,
And for every sing-song of Sweetie! Babe! Angel!
She waits for the One Who Will Come Back
The one who will notice her red sequin dress,
The one who will get her higher than high.

A lone car descends from way up high
Above the hill. Would this one hold love,
The money for another sequin dress?
The car slows and turns on its dome light.
She turns her back
From the car she hears the name, Angel.

"Wanna go for a ride, Angel?"
The man repeats his high-
pitched snarl. She turns back
to the car. Could this be love?
Had she finally seen the light
To take off her dress?

He's playing with the fringe of her dress
From the window of the car, "I'll call you Angel,
Okay, Babe?" She enters the light
of the car. Her high-
lights brush his skanky arm. "Gonna love where I take
        you Angel, you might not want to come back.

She wonders if there is time to turn back.
Could she change her dress,
Change her mind. Forget about love,
At least the kind from her Angel.
Could she stop trying to feel the high?
Could she move from the light?

"Oh mother Angel, dress me in love
and white light. Bring me back
To earth. I no longer want to be high."

Part II

No need for tear drops.
He'd watch them fall on her chest.
Like all boys,
Wishing he could own all girls.
Doing anything so he could have it.
So much money, so much fucking

He mumbles to her about fucking
While he takes some money and drops
The bills on the seat, so she can see them.
She places the cash by her chest.
She gets in the car, like most girls.
He speeds off into the dark. Like most boys.

"Angel, you love boys,
Don't you? Just like you love fucking."
He breathes this into her ear. He hates girls
She can tell. He then drops
His hands to touch her chest.
If this could only be it.

But this is never just it.
He opens his fly, and plays with his boys
And pokes and probes her chest.
This is what he calls pre-fucking
His fist drops
To make sure she is like all girls.

To him she resembles all girls.
Now he has the green light to do it.
He pushes her on all fours and drops
His pants. To be one of the good ol' boys,
The world is just fucking.
As he pulls her dress up to her chest.

Friction plants weeping willows in her chest.
He's done this before to many girls,
And she knows it. No love, just everyday fucking.
She's done this before, and he knows it.
He finishes quickly like all boys
And leaves. She's lost in the darkness,
        tears, sweat, and semen drops.

Here here, Father Fucking, you are all boys,
Wanting everything from all girls! Your tiny drops
Of liquid love never make it into my hope chest.

Laurel Barclay

Laurel Barclay was born and raised in Greenwich Village, New York. She attended PS 3, an ultraliberal elementary school, and went to Secular Jewish Humanist Communist! Summer Camp. Even at the most progressive school on earth Laurel was often in trouble for disobeying authority and flashing the boys. During this period she began a journalism career with *Children's Express*, an internationally syndicated news service with the motto, "By Children For Everybody." Her coverage of the Democratic election campaign in 1988 won her an Emmy award for "Outstanding Coverage in a News and Documentary Series." Buzz Aldrin presented this award to her, so she has touched a man who was on the moon.

In 5th grade Laurel's teacher Lucy taught her that to write a poem you first put down all your ideas and then eliminate all the unnecessary words. It was then that Laurel understood she was a poet.

In her private Quaker junior high school experience, Laurel learned about rich people, sex and drugs, began classical vocal training, met Matthew Katz-Bohen and read *Night* by Eli Weisel. John Burns, her 8th-grade literature teacher, introduced her to the concept that still strongly influences her work today: "Every generation is equidistant from barbarism."

Unable to attend the Bronx High School of Science out of rebelliousness and boredom, Laurel spent years pacing 8th Street as well as singing, talking, writing and experimenting in Strawberry Fields, Washington Square Park, The Waverly Diner, Café LaFortuna, etc. Here she formed many lifelong friendships and developed as an artist. She ended up at City-As-High School and took her first "perfpo" class at the New School for Social Research with the notorious Bob Holman. A natural exhibitionist, Laurel took to performing immediately and "slammed" at the Nuyorican Poets Café.

Laurel found that melody expressed what she could not express with words alone. She formed various bands collaborating with men who played instruments and inspired her lyrics and singing. At 16 she formed her first band, Variety City with Matthew Katz-Bohen and Giorgio Handman. Matthew became her lover and greatest musical partner and they continue to work and sleep together today.

Laurel attended college and formed the band DADDY with Matt. Matt originally rejected the band name DADDY but Laurel firmly believed, "Too many people in today's world do not have a Daddy. Now you can scream 'I love you Daddy' and mean it," so the name stuck.

Extensive touring and independent promotion have landed DADDY features in *Paper* magazine, *Interview* magazine, and *Q* magazine. They have been in Levi's advertisements, Anna Sui's runway show, ESPN's X-Games, Japanese TV shows and newspapers, the award-winning documentary *Freaks, Glam Gods and Rock Stars*, a commercial promoting the Grammy Awards on CBS, the Howl Festival in which they scored the music and performed in a play by Ed Sanders of the FUGS, and lots of other stuff.

In 2005 Laurel and Matt have The Songwriters Hall of Fame Abe Olman Scholarship for Excellence in Songwriting, put out their fourth album, *The Beast: LIVE* on the independent label Germ Music, and have a single coming out in the UK on Only Lovers Left Alive records.

Poetry

I want to write some great poetry today
But I would kind of rather watch TV
Take sedatives and masturbate and sleep
Alternately in my bed all day long

If you die

If you die in the water you should be allowed to stay
there while the fishes eat you but they will take you out
of your watery death and dry you off put the body in a
box and put the box in the dirt.

Airplane Crash

Airplane crash like beautiful sunrise
Big explosion fire is beautiful
The factory is leaking delicious perfume
Prostitutes with only one I
I can't see anything at all
I took so many pretty pills
Airplanes crashing

It's my birthday

Utter terror
Utter terror
Utter terror
It's my birthday
Utter terror
Bloody party
Endless weekday
It's my birthday

Woke up with my mind
Went back to sleep
Woke up with my mind
It is bright
I am awake
And I can see that
Because I'm blind
And out of bed

Utter terror
Utter terror
Bloody party
Endless day
Utter terror
It's my birthday

He takes his shoes off

He takes his shoes off
He takes his pants off
She thinks he's so tough
She knows he'll be rough
One bullet is all it takes
Can't stop myself
It's never hard enough
It's never good enough
You're never satisfied
Until you die
One bullet is all it takes

(This poem is meant to describe the relationship
between orgasm and suicide: sex is never very satisfying
and neither is life)

Suicide Pills

Give me suicide pills
Over the counter
Give me suicide pills
Die when I want to
Die when I want to
They make it hard for you
I just want to die
I just want to die when I want to

Sleeplessness

The morning works like this, there are two options and
the mixture of the two to choose from if you are me:
Consciousness occurs suddenly as if there was no sleep
to wake up from. Excitement inexplicable twittering in
the light. If there are other sleeping humans nearby
they squint cruelly and frown. The optimism and enthu-
siasm is quickly turned to aimless   uncomfortable
useless unnecessary   superfluous and annoying
manic exhaustion. The new day begins.

Option Two the less frequent of the two sometimes the
only option. Consciousness comes on abruptly reversing
the serenity of sleep if there was any. Inexplicable panic
and blues in the lucid lighting. Nobody stirs. Only rest-
lessness drives the body from this warm bed an unre-
strainable force uprights the being for the new day has
begun.

I had great sex

I had great sex
With a Corona bottle
I had my period and it was
Bloody
I had great sex with a
Corona bottle and then
Somebody told me
That I could have sucked out my insides

Rat love

I have a pet and now I have rat love
So now I worry that my rat is going to die
Like the plants that I killed decaying in the corner
I don't want to be someone who kills
But I guess I can be
My rat loves to love me
Climb in my neck and sniff my ears
Today he had soft shit
Not the usual pellets
Maybe it's just stress
He was just a rat and now he's
The love of my life
I know it's hard to love me
I need a lot
But if he has to be alone to be okay
Well then I won't touch him

R.I.P. Sergio, January–March 1999

Eternally

My aging mother is tied to my back and getting
    decrepiter

Dreaming of a friend who died in the summer

I killed Nick Bohn and I don't remember doing it
But now I have his body in this bag and it looks like
    black balls of tar lumped together
I need to hide the body so I won't get in trouble but I
    can't find a good place to put it and
I keep dropping clumps of it

A very nice dream that I had a brand new baby

my brand new baby sucking on my left breast
feels so good I am aroused, relaxed and happy
I put the baby to sleep in a sling made out of soft net
    and I hang it on the doorknob
it holds the baby in a little ball like in the womb
I wanted to make love to my man but I was bleeding
    too much because I had had a baby
so I just enjoyed the baby sucking my right breast

Anticar

So nice and clean like baby tushies
Sky dream clean
Highways going eighty miles per hour
Gas price hike war

So nice and green
The trees and bushes
Sky dream clean
Highways going eighty miles per hour
Gas price hike war
GAS PRICE HIKE
WAR

So many sounds of baby animals
Live in my dreams
Highways going eighty miles per hour
Gas price hike war
So many sounds are disappearing
Like ghosts in a dream
They should ring everafter
everafter everafter

Come take a ride in The Anticar
Come take a ride in The Anticar
Is there a beyond petroleum?
Is there a beyond beyond beyond beyond beyond
    beyond beyond beyond

Tranny smile

I can't deny that you are gone
There is a hole inside my groin
Empty space inside my head
My head is filled with
Woe
Woe woe woe woe
Tranny smile

A dream

I'm not sure if you were there yet
But at least I was learning how to
Transport my fish. A large experienced
Man showed me how to hollow out the
Center of an onion because that would be the
Best travel environment for my pets.
I took the insides out of a small but healthy
Onion and then I lost track of it. The other onions were
Rotten. I carved them out anyway hoping that it would
Be possible to cover the holes with Saran Wrap or
Aluminum foil. The tall and big man thought I was
An idiot and told me to forget about it, he would do it
Himself he said and smiled an upsetting liar's grin
And I knew my fish were not safe

Then you were there and we were moving
To a locked ward with the craziest.
The playroom had multi levels where the
Mental patients stood on platforms

Displayed like go-go dancers at a disco.
Elizabeth Frank my old college advisor and
A Pulitzer Prize–winning biographer played
The supervisor and she asked us first if we were violent
And second if we liked to cook.
I said we were not really violent and I could see
In her eyes that she was sure at least I was.
Then I said we like to cook, he likes to cook.
Oh good she said and handed you a knife
Which you immediately used to chop a large
Amount of onions. Then Liz started talking
About her two children: "the adopted one always
Wants me to tell her she's not real. It is so sad
Nobody cares that she's not really a child it's her
        attitude
Makes me feel so angry." When Liz said that
Or something like that I realized how much sicker
She was than me.

Last night I had an awful dream that started out nice and beautiful

looking into the sea by the shore there is this huge shell
        with all kinds of snails and plants and fish living in it
trying to touch it but this big crab keeps pinching me,
he is fast and can get me however I turn or move
it doesn't hurt that bad but I have to shake him against
        the rocks to get him off my finger
and he finally drives me away from his spot
I am happy and impressed by this crab's strength,
        willfulness and loyal protection of his beautiful
        territory

I told Matt about him but he already knew of the
   tenacious crab
We went back to see him and he was standing boldly
   guarding his turf.

Matt said, "Why does the crab have a sad face?"

I looked and part of the shell on his face was broken off

It was very sad

I tried to make it okay by telling myself that that is what
   happens to brave fighters

Howler monkey

I am a howler monkey and I swing fast and strong from
   tree to tree in the
cool wet morning air
howling
The sound rings for miles in the forest

There are no trees and my arms and tail are weak in
   this city
A howl can't be heard above the sounds of cars

Having all these bloody fucking bloody sex images running through my mind's eyes

A vision:
Arms stretched out
Slit from wrist to elbow
Blood pouring
From mouth
Eyes
Pussy
Arms gushing
Walking towards me

But I see it both ways
My eyes are in the naked bloody body
And I am watching her walk towards me

The image is hot

My breasts feel soft under my clean cotton shirt

I was walking in Central Park near 59th Street Columbus Circle

I was walking in Central Park near 59th Street
Columbus Circle and it was very crowded and bustling
as it always is on a weekday afternoon. My legs were
very tight and heavy and achy and I could barely walk
each step was a struggle. All of a sudden a car from the
street crashed full speed into a tree in the park. An
Arab family got out of the wreck and stood staring at all
the people. Everyone panicked and dropped to the
ground screaming and covering their heads. We all
thought that a bomb would go off and kill us and I was
terrified. After a few minutes nothing happened and we
all got up and started to leave I was very bewildered
and scared. I kept thinking that this was the final straw
and I could no longer live in New York. I was confused
and ended up entering a deli near by. I stared at the
beverages in the case and chose an Amstel Light beer. I
needed a drink. I told the cashier and the other cus-
tomers what had just gone on in the park and sat down
at a table with a few patrons eating their lunch and told
them about it. One woman had tuna sushi but there
must have been 5 pounds of tuna on her plate. I said
"You're going to go home and grill the rest of it
tonight."

The beast

I am the Beast
I am the Feast
Call me by my name baby!

I am the Beast
I am the Feast

Even as they strike you down
Remember
Man is not our enemy
Hatred will never let you face
The beast inside us
Man is not the enemy

In the grass there is a snake
Crawling in silence
Waits for the time to eat the bird
Ggrrrooow
Hatred will never let you face
The beast inside us
Man is not the enemy

I am the Beast
I am the Feast
Call me by my name baby!

I am the Beast
I am the Feast

Giggly wiggly

You make me feel all wriggly
You make me giggly wiggly
You make me bouncy bumpy
You make me jerky turkey

Watching you from my window
Your walk is making me horny
You frying eggs on the sidewalk
Just clicking your heels on the pavement

You got me all ignited
You got me so excited
Your body's licky sticky
Baby please tell me you feel me

My heart is all a flutter
Got some something dirty to mutter
You make me yummy cummy
You make me cummy yummy

Your love is like the sun
No tree can shelter me
And you start to turn me on
FLAMMABILITY

Your body is so hot
Hot enough to roast an ox
The fire gets too hot for me
FLAMMABILITY

An american nightmare

So lonely the monster sits counting his money drinking
and peeing.

Poetry saves

Show me the way to your heart and I'll play the part
    tonight
All of the faces I see in the club distort in the light
Spinning so fast on the floor don't you see I need more
    that is right
Wait for the darkness I wait for the darkness to shut out
    the light
The club is my last religion I come crawling on bended
    knee
God is my DJ the poetry he plays will resurrect me
Sex and martinis they mix can the lonely ever be free
Shutting my eyes and drinking away the misery
Music come save us tonight we are dancing away the
    pain
Come let the poetry control you go right in your soul
    babe
Come let me touch you and hold you and I will console
    your pain
Poetry come save us tonight we are dancing away all of
    the pain

Used by you

You never wanted to baby but I made you make me cry
You always treat me so badly but I beg you to hurt me
　　　every time
When I wake up in the morning there is no one by my
　　　side
I like it better that way please taste the bitter tears I cry
I want to be used by you
Look in the thunder and lightning revealing the dark
　　　side of your mind
I see a place deep within all a place where the mean
　　　man cannot hide
This love was meant to be I should have known it from
　　　the start
I like the way that is feels when you stick your knife
　　　into my heart
Tie the shackles tighter it's the only way I feel
Kick me punch me bite me pain is the only thing that's
　　　real

Love is the beginning of the end

It started in the winter
Trying to stay warm it all began
There were no more flowers
Everything I touched
Died in my hands
I need to know
Will you be here when I go?

Now it's getting warmer
Tiny birds are singing in the sky
Everything is melting
I wipe the sleep out of my eyes
Is it true?
I will always be with you

Love is the beginning of the end
Love is the beginning of the end
Love is the beginning of the end of the beginning of
    the end of the beginning of the end
The End

In the middle of the summer
Feeling heavy with the heat
Lying with you naked
Kicking off the sheets
I need to know
Will you be here in the snow?

It is cold now
Everything is falling to the ground
The love from last December
Is nowhere to be found

Oh is it true?
I will always be with you

Love is the beginning of the end
Love is the beginning of the end
Love is the beginning of the end of the beginning of
     the end of the beginning of the end

Sold again and again

21st Century Slaves
are not hard to keep
they don't need no food
don't need no sleep
open up the door
see what we've found
bodies on the floor
they don't make a sound

I can't sleep
They tell me to go home but
There isn't any bread
I want to be my own but
I'm sold again
And again

Bird crazy

My mother likes to feed the birds
I like to see them fly in the distance
My gramma likes to feed the birds
So high up like little insects
I like to hear them scream in the sky

CAW CAW COO KOO CA CA
        CREEEEEEEEKEEEEcookoocac

When my mom was ten she had birds
They had eggs and she loved them
They were all born wet and deformed
They all died and she was scarred
They never got to scream in the sky

CAW CAW CAW cookoo coocoo CAW CAW
        CREEEREEEee CAAAAk

Oh COME ON BIRDS
You know you want to be a bird
You know you want to be a sea gull
Flying in the sky

Hoo Hoo Hoo
You are dreaming you are a bird
You are dreaming you can fly
You are dreaming you are a bird
You are dreaming you can fly

Hoo Hoo Hoo Hoo

FILES OF NASTY THINGS (A-Z
Attorneys-beer-cigarettes)
        Memory   a foul lingering old onion
                        Spoiled   beef   mind

ONE MONSTER SICK OF IT ALL
    Smacks another zombie in the face
                    both lose
    one head rolls   one arm sloughs off

I hope I am not old and lonely walking my prick like a
    poodle.

For Ozzy Osbourne (my favorite)

Tell me people am I going insane
Asked Ozzy and then he cried like a little baby
No Ozzy baby you're still sane I wanna tell him
Over breakfast soft boiled eggs in cups tea

Dawn for the loser

Sitting on the pier
The only one there
I cannot sleep
I cannot pay for it
Dirt wind blowing my filthy hair

Atlantic City put a hole in me
One cup of coffee in the cold
One dollar bill in the river
Thank god the sunrise is free

He gave me another day
He didn't take my life away
He gave me another day
He didn't take my life away
He gave me another day
He didn't take my life away
He gave me another day
He didn't take my life away

Sitting on the pier
The only one there
I cannot sleep
I cannot pay for it
Dirt wind blowing my filthy hair

Fantasy song

Long nice cool day with you
Talking and fucking don't matter what's happening
We can walk in the grass
Lay naked all day in bed with you

Oh I love making love all drunk and high with you
You make me laugh all day

Please stay make love to me more at dawn
Your sweet face in the sun so quiet at dawn
Talk to me about everything

Oh I love making love to you
You make me laugh

Feed It

Too bored to eat my food
Wish it all came in pill form
And take my eyes out
Take my eyes out

Drinking without drinking
Intravenous drinking
Thinking with out thinking
Intravenous thinking

Gotta force feed it or it won't eat it
Force feed it or it won't eat it

Too tired to fall in love
Wish it all came in pill form
And take my mind out
Take my mind out

Thinking without drinking
Intravenous drinking
Thinking drinking thinking
Thinking thinking thinking

Grey children

Grey children in the factory
Brick wall flourescent lights
Machines no air to breathe
Grey children
    in the factory

How can you grow up

How can you grow up
    to have grey children

Wheres all the twees go?
Wheres all the twees go?

    Asphalt highway plastic highway

Grey children no flowers to pick no sun in the sky no
    trees
Grey children no butterfly no birds in the sky

Lions eat gazelles

Sometimes mothers kill their kids
Kids kill other kids
Fathers kill their wives
We all kill ourselves
I'm a vicious sister
Her brother kicks her
Sell the stupid baby
Kill em all ourselves
And lions eat gazelles

Rats fucking
Half dead bees caught in spider's webs
Struggling in spider's webs
Ha ha ha ha ha ha ha

Of course
You just wanna cause pain
Bite people eat their brains
Make them die cut them up
See them bloody all fucked up
Ha ha ha ha ha ha ha ha ha

Politics

I don't want no stupid boyfriend
Men are stupid and annoying
Always beating and raping girls
I don't want no stupid boyfriend

All my experience with boys
They want mommy I'm not mommy
They break guns and come in your hair
Shove their cocks down your throat
I don't want no stupid boyfriend

But there's this one
There's this one and He knows everything
He wants to be me He knows everything
And He eats my pussy for as long as I want him to
He eats my pussy for as long as I want him to

Showdown

The mood is ugly
High noon
The sky is red
Blood and doom
Walking steady
Real slow
Blood thirsty
Showdown
Pocket full of bullets
Head filled up with rage
Everybody knows how
Murders is made

An affair between a woman and the oceanman

Bring me to the sea
Tie me to the sand
Let the water wash over me
Take me in his hand

The sweet love we're making you won't forget
The beauty of death
Brings us closer

Don't wake up
Don't wake up
With the ocean in your hair
Baby, stay with me
Stay with me
Stay with me
Stay with me

You were walking and you were following me
Down to the unknown
Down
Down
Down
Down
Down
You were walking and you were following me
Down
Drown
Drown
Drown

You never know
You never know
Until you go

Gary Mex Glazner

Gary Mex Glazner makes his living as a poet. In the early days of the Bowery Poetry Club, Glazner would fill in as needed for club owner Bob Holman; this led to Glazner's title of "Temporary Bob." HarperCollins, W.W. Norton and Salon.com have published his work. His poetry performances have been featured on CNN, NPR and underwater on the Bay Area Rapid Transit System. He is the author of *Ears on Fire: Snapshot Essays in a World of Poets*, published by La Alameda Press; the book chronicles a year abroad in Asia and Europe meeting poets, working on translations and writing poems. His book, *How to Make a Living as a Poet*, with Soft Skull Press, features essays on creative poetry programming and interviews with leading poets and gives bookstores a myriad of ways to display the book, including under fantasy, science fiction, blank books and mystery.

Glazner is the director of the Alzheimer's Poetry Project (APP) which has been featured on NBC's "Today" and NPR's "Weekend Edition." A simple idea: members of APP read to patients classic poems that they might have learned while young. Even in the late stages of the disease this helps spark memories so they often say words and lines along with the reader.

Glazner is poet-in-residence and coach of the Precision Poetry Drill Team at Desert Academy in Santa Fe; the team was featured on NPR's "All Things Considered." He is the editor of the "Word Art: Poetry Broadside" series, at the Palace of the Governors Museum, where he sets type and runs the old printing presses. Glazner has lectured on Federico García Lorca for the Santa Fe Opera. He, with co-producer Don McIver, won the 2004 Special Merit Award from the National Federation of Community Broadcasters, for "The Poetry of Vietnam," which was broadcast on KUNM in Albuquerque. Glazner is the host of "Poetry Talk," on KSFR in Santa Fe.

Denise Kusel of *The Santa Fe New Mexican* says, "Poet Gary Mex Glazner belies a mild manner with an inyourface delivery. He shouts. He postures. He's a madman, insisting you get it—all of it. Because he holds nothing back he's insightful and dangerous, as only a good poet can be."

Can Poetry Drinks Matter?

Ingredients:
1 oz Dana Gioia
1/2 oz Green crème de menthe
1/2 oz White crème de menthe
1/2 oz Cream
4 Olives

Mixing Instructions:
Get ee cummings to juggle the olives while Langston
Hughes shakes the martini glass and Anne Sexton rum-
bas. After clearing the bathtub of O'Hara and Ginsberg,
invite the rest of the posse (Dickinson, Wheatley, Poe
and Simic and Longfellow [do not forget Longfellow!])
to squeeze in. Fill tub to brim. Hold it right there,
Poet! NO DRINKING till everyone gets here! Except
for you, of course. It matters. No ideas but in cham-
pagne flutes.

The *Billy Collins*

You are the 2 oz Gin
You are the 1 oz Lemon juice
You are the 1 tsp Superfine sugar
I am the 3 oz Club soda
I am the Maraschino cherry
I am the slice Orange
But don't worry I am not the 2 oz Gin
You are still the 2 oz Gin
Not to mention the 1 oz Lemon juice
And—somehow—
The Superfine sugar.

William Burroughs' Naked Lunch Punch

Ingredients:
Bottle Midori melon liqueur
1/2 pint Peachtree schnapps
6 pack of Sprite or 7-Up (shaken)
1/4 pint Heavy cream

Mixing Instructions:
Pour into large bowl.
Place bowl on top of head.
Pray for good aim.

Richard Brautigan's Trout Drinking in America

Ingredients:
1 mint-green Maraschino cherry sans stem
1/2 oz Jägermeister
1 package of Kool-Aid
Ocean

Mixing Instructions:
Place green cherry in mouth.
Slam shot of Jägermeister.
Place package of Kool-Aid
in ocean, notice it becomes
"mere shadow of its desired potency."

Repeat.

The *Karen Finley*

1 shot Amaretto
1 shot Southern Comfort
Ice cubes
Yam

The *Hart Crane*

> *"Just once I saw Crane swimming strongly, but*
> *never again."*
>
> *Gertrude Vogt*

2 oz Brandy (Courvoisier)
1-1/2 oz Grand Marnier
Juice of 1/2 Lemon
Ice cubes
Sugar
Candle

Place ingredients in brandy snifter.
Light candle, drink.
Then drop by drop, let out a perfect cry.

The *Samuel Beckett* Nothing To Be Done

1-1/2 oz Apricot brandy
1 tsp Gin
1 tbsp Light cream

Wait

The *Jack Kerouac* Satori in Paris

1-1/2 oz Gin
1 tsp Anis
1 tsp Light cream
1 Egg white

Mixing instructions:
Somewhere during my ten days in Paris I received an illumination of some kind that seems to've changed me again, towards what I suppose'll be my pattern for another seven years or more: in effect, a satori: the Japanese word for "sudden illumination," "sudden awakening" or simply "kick in the eye."—Whatever. . .

The Beowulf

Ingredients:
1-1/4 oz Captain Morgan's rum
3/4 oz Orange Curaçao
1-1/4 oz Sweet and sour mix
1-1/2 oz Tequila
3/4 oz Triple sec
3/4 oz Lime juice

Mixing instructions:
Drink this and chant: Gyrede hine BééëWuuulf
Drink more. Chant more. Understand more.

The *Robert Frosty*

1-1/2 oz Vodka
Fill with Clamato juice
3 dashes Tabasco sauce
3 dashes Worcestershire sauce (optional)

Mixing instructions:
I think I know enough of spice,
To say Tabasco will suffice.
It also might be nice
To add some cubes of ice.
Garnish with forked celery stick,
And that will make all the difference.

The *Coleridge*

1 oz Barenjager
1 oz Rumple Minze
1 oz Jägermeister
1 lump Opium

Mixing instructions:
Smoke opium. Forget everything.

The *Wanda Coleman*

> *Dark bars are female, sumptuous holes, sometimes*
> *stark, dense atmospheres*
> *with smells thick as menstrual blood.*

1-1/2 oz Light rum
Juice of 1/2 Lime
1 tsp Powdered sugar

Mixing instructions:
Shake all ingredients with ice,
strain into a cocktail glass,
and get down on it.

Rilke's The Drunkard's Song

> *It wasn't in me. It went out and in.*
> *I wanted to hold it.*

1/2 oz Butterscotch schnapps
1/4 oz Green crème de menthe
1/4 oz Bailey's Irish cream
1/4 oz Grenadine

Mixing instructions:
. . . but there are many more faces, because
each person has several of them . . .
drink and see how many you see.

The *Anne Waldman*

1-1/2 oz Dark crème de cacao
1/2 oz Vodka
1 tsp Chocolate syrup
1 tsp Cherry brandy
1 fresh Peyote button
1 Skull

Mixing instructions:
Eat peyote. Pour ingredients into skull. Puke.
Ask bartender to chant "Fast Speaking Woman" slowly.
Chant along until vision becomes reality.

The *Neruda*

> *They are not reached by the wine bullet. . .*

1/3 Gin
1/3 Whisky
1/3 Pernod

Mixing instructions:
Drink up! Celebrate
residence on earth!

The *Mary Oliver*

1/5 oz Dark rum
1/5 oz Kahlua
1/5 oz Amaretto
2/5 oz Bailey's Irish Cream

Mixing instructions:
Serve with fried moles and skunk cabbage.

The Fancy *Bly*

2 oz Gin
1/4 tsp Triple sec
1/4 tsp Powdered sugar
1 dash Bitters
1 twist Lemon peel

Mixing instructions:
Shake ingredients as all men pound bar.
Pound it like a drum.

The *Paul Muldoon*

Glass of Irish whiskey

Mixing instructions:
Stir with a wink and a wink and a winkie-wick
Or substitute a stink and stink and a stinky-stick and
      drinky, drink.

The *Ted Kooser*

1 Glass of water
1 Field of wheat

Mixing instructions:
Don't.
Sip and stare.

The *C. K. Williams*

1 shot Chambord raspberry liqueur
1 shot Vodka
Fill with Soda water

Mixing instructions:
Drink all at once through the straw . . . though in truth
I can't imagine what; reality
has put itself so solidly
before me there's little need for mystery . . .

The *Robert Creeley*

One bottle of bourbon
One night

Mixing instructions:
Talks, even if finally
to no one,
talks and talks.

The *Guillaume Apollinaire*

1-1/2 oz Gin
1-1/2 oz red Dubonnet
1 dash Angostura bitters

Mixing instructions:
DRINK
RINKD
INKDR
NKDRI
KDRIN

The *Anna Akhmatova*

One bottomless bottle of Vodka

Mixing instructions:
Have each one of your friends memorize a line of your
        poetry,
destroy all copies of your poems,
collect your friends in a book.

Li Po-Three Way

1 cup of wine
1 flowering tree
1 drinker
0 friend
1 bright moon,
1 shadow—makes three.

Mixing Instructions:
The moon, shit, is no drinker of wine.
Have shadow creep about
Is moon friend? (what about that time?)
Is shadow slave? (remember to ask)
Make merry—spend Spring
Sing songs—moon
Drunk three shared the fun;
Now each goes own way.
When see each other, pretend It didn't happen.

The *Gary Snyder*

3/4 oz Cherry brandy
3/4 oz Gin
3/4 oz Yellow Chartreuse

Mixing instructions:
Kill a deer. Stir
all ingredients with ice,
strain into an old wine
skin, and serve.

The *Langston Hughes*

1 raisin
1 sun
1/2 pound rotten meat
1 cup Karo syrup

Mixing instructions:
Pick at festering sore.
Shake until it explodes.

Tennessee Williams' Hint o' Mint

4 ounces Bourbon whiskey
4 to 6 Sprigs of mint
2 Sugar cubes

Mixing instructions:
Put bourbon, mint, and sugar into the bottom of a
    cocktail shaker.
Muddle to dissolve sugar and blend mint leaves.
Let stand for a bit to help release the mint flavor.
Add ice, shake well to chill, then strain into a glass filled
    with shaved ice.
Yell "Stella!" and drink.

The *Dylan Thomas*

18 Whiskies

Mixing Instructions:
It turns out that Thomas drank only 8 whiskies and actually was suffering from pneumonia, which his doctor misdiagnosed. Thinking him to be having delirium tremens he then injected the poet with three doses of morphine. After the third dose, Thomas's face turned blue and he sank into a coma. Sure his poor health and drinking contributed to the pneumonia, but it was his boast of drinking the 18 whiskies that led the doctor to his misdiagnosis. Well. I, for one, am glad we got that cleared up. (Info from *Dylan Remembered 1935–1953*, David Thomas and Dr. Simon Barton.)

Rage, rage against the boasting
of what you drank last night.

The *Shakespeare*

1 Stage
1 World
A bunch of Men and women
(Note exits and entrances in case of fire)
1 Infant mewling
1 School boy whining
1 Lover (add woeful ballad to taste)
1 quick Solider
1 Cannon's mouth
1 Justice (preferably with round belly, can use pillow if
    necessary)
1 wise Saw
1 Pantaloon
1 pair Spectacles
1 side Pouch
1 pair youthful Hose
1 shrunk Shank

Mixing Instructions:
Puke in nurse's arms, creep like snail, sigh like furnace,
beard like pard, quote a few modern instances, shift
into sixth age, save hose, squeeze big manly voice
through sieve, place pipes and whistles in sound, take
strange eventful history, crush with second childishness,
subtract teeth, subtract eyes, subtract taste, subtract
everything.

The *Edna St. Vincent Millay*

1 Candle

Mixing Instructions:
Light both ends.

The *Willam Blake*

1 Tyger

Mixing Instructions:
Light both ends.

The *Patti Smith*

1 Baby
1 Black sheep

Mixing Instructions:
Get Baby big, get baby get bigger.
Get Baby, get something, get Baby get more.
Baby, baby, baby was a rock-and-roll nigger.
Look around you, all around you,
Riding copper wave.
Behave.

The *Lou Reed*

1 Holly
1 Pair plucked eyebrows
2 Pair shaved her legs
1 Walk
1 wild Side
1 Candy from out on the Island
3 Colored girls
1 Doo do doo do doo do do doo
1 Little Joe
1 Sugar Plum Fairy
1 Jackie

Mixing Instructions:
Hitch-hike across the USA, go he to she, go to back-room, be everybody's darlin'. Don't lose your head, even when giving head, take walk, repeat as neccessary.

The *Ntozake Shange*

2 measures Tequila
Orange juice
2 dashes Grenadine

Mixing instructions:
lady in brown-shake, lady in yellow-shake, lady in
    purple-shake,
lady in red-shake, lady in green-shake, lady in blue-
    shake,
lady in orange-shake, enuf.

The *Sharon Olds*

1 cup spicy Bloody Mary mix
1 cup fresh squeezed Orange juice
1/2 cup fresh squeezed Lime juice
3 teaspoons Grenadine
Dash Chili powder
Pinch of Salt
Fresh ground Pepper

Mixing instructions:
Combine all ingredients with naked body on sheet. Add
sweat jumping out of pores, stir well with palm. Serve
on belly. Sign on for duration.

The *Diane Wakoski*

1/2 ounce Vodka
1/2 ounce Kahlua
1/4 ounce Irish Cream liqueur

Mixing instructions:
Combine with cracked ice in a shaker. Shake
as you dance on the grave of a son of a bitch.

The Sassy *Aptowicz*

250 ml Grenadine
1/8 gal Lemonade
1 L Squirt
2 splashes Lime juice
1 pint Triple sec
3 splashes Margarita mix

Mixing instructions:
Put ingredients into cocktail shaker,
Duct tape shaker to ass, mix vigorously, shout "Sassy, sassy, sassy!" until sassified.

The *Reggie Gibson*

1/2 shot Blue Curaçao
Champagne

Mixing instructions:
Top up Blue Curaçao with Champagne.
Garnish with a grape or strawberry, light candle,
whisper daggers and moonbeams
of loves convulsing paroxysms.

The *Anne Sexton*

2 oz Gin
1/2 oz Vermouth
1 bottle Knockout drops

Mixing instructions:
Stir over ice and strain into a chilled cocktail glass, garnish with a spear of olives, put on striped dress, mix with knockout drops, sleep.

Fuggy *Sanders*

1 ounce Vodka
1 ounce Peach schnapps
4 ounces Orange juice

Mixing instructions:
Pour ingredients into a highball glass almost filled with
ice. Levitate Pentagon.

The *Edward Learbanger*

1-1/2 ounces Vodka
1 ounce Galliano
Chilled Orange juice
Lemon slice
1 Owl
1 Pussy cat

Mixing instructions:
Pour vodka and Galliano over ice in a highball glass.
Top up with orange juice. Garnish with lemon slice. Sail
away for a year and a day to the land where the bong
tree grows, sing o lovely pussy, o pussy my love, what a
beautiful pussy you are, you are, you are . . . works best
at closing time.

The *Roethke* Sour

1-1/2 oz Whiskey
5 oz Sour mix
1 tbsp Maraschino cherry juice
2 dashes Bitters

Mixing instructions:
Shake and strain onto breath, make a small boy dizzy;
hang on like death; waltz, decorate with a red cherry.

Hot Buttered *Longfellow*

1 teaspoon powdered Sugar
1/2 cup boiling Water
1/4 cup Rum
1 tbsp Butter
Freshly grated Nutmeg
An Arrow

Mixing instructions:
Place powdered sugar in a hot tumbler and add boiling
water, rum and butter. Stir well and sprinkle nutmeg on
top. Shoot an arrow in the air. Run like hell, you know
not where.

A *Brian Wilson*

3/4 oz Triple sec
3/4 oz Gin
1 tbsp Pineapple juice
One bunch Vibrations
One peck Excitations

Mixing instructions:
Vibrate all ingredients, strain into a little deuce coupe
and chug-a-lug.

1001 Ways to Draft a Beer

Ask Tuli Kupferberg

The *Ted Joans*

1/2 glass Guinness
1/2 glass cheap Champagne

Mixing instructions:
So you want to be hip little squares
So take a sip
Leave a tip
Say yes more often

Bob Kaufman's Jazzy Chick Drink

2 parts (lemon infused) Vodka
1 part Cointreau
2–3 parts Cranberry juice
Squeezed lemon or lime
Lemon slice
Golden sardine

Mixing instructions:
Stir or shake with ice and strain into a chilled martini
    glass.
Garnish with a slice of lemon, take vow of silence.
Garnish with golden sardine.

Gregory Corso's Bomb

Pour equal amounts of sambuca and a cream liqueur of
    your choice (Dooley's, Bailey's Irish Cream . . .)
    into a shot glass.
Layer a dash of grenadine on top (pour over the back of
    a spoon).

Drink, stand on bar and BOOM BOOM
    BOOM BOOM

"Poet's Eye Obscenely Drinking"
(*Ferlinghetti* Punch)

Red wine
White wine
Fruits of the season (oranges, apples, grapes)
Sprite/7-Up, cola and orange soda (Fanta)

Mixing instructions:
Mix with one third red wine, one third white wine and
    one third mixed sodas.
Add fruit and ice.

Best served on Coney Island, in big wine glasses, drink
    surface of round world, throw in drugged store
    cowboys and Las Vegas virgins,
careful of the sunbathers.

The *Fernando Pessoa*

1 bottle of Port
6 Glasses

Mixing instructions:
Fill glasses. Drink with heteronyms.

The *Marc Smith*

12 cups of Coffee, black

Mixing instructions:
So What!

The *Bob Holman*

1 Poetry Club
1 Full Bar

Mixing instructions:
Carve jade flute, make it gold, make it beautiful as a
bottle of wine. Make bottle a woman. Fill self and oth-
ers with poetry and wine, laugh, drop pen, end poem.
Will it bring wealth and fame? Ask the bartender!

The *Sonia Sanchez*

2 ounces White rum
1/2 ounce Lime juice
1 teaspoon Sugar
6 whole Mint leaves
2 ounces Soda water

Mixing instructions:
Put juice and sugar into a highball glass and sashay. Rub
mint leaves on body until you feel human, human,
human huhuhuhuhuhuhuman. Fill with crushed ice
and rum, stir.

Edgar Allan Poe's The Raven

1 part midnight dreary Grand Marnier
1 part weak Kahlua
1 part weary Bailey's Irish Cream
1 Raven

Mixing instructions:
Gently tap ingredients, then nod, nap, rap, quote, with
ice, quoth,   strain, whisper Lenore, into tumblers or
serve as shooters. Nevermore.

The *Amiri Baraka*

2 oz Vodka
Dash extra dry Vermouth

Mixing instructions:
Stir gently

The *Osip Mandelstam*

1-1/2 oz Vodka
1/2 oz Coffee liqueur
1/2 oz Cream

Mixing instructions:
Wait for guests you love, serve, rattle door in its chains.

The *Etheridge Knight*

3/4 oz Light rum
3/4 oz Dark rum
1 oz Pineapple juice
1 oz Orange juice
1 oz Lemon juice
1 tsp. powdered Sugar
Dash overproof Rum ("151")

Mixing instructions:
Tape 47 photos of ancestors to wall, take your place among them.

Jorge Luis Borges' Alephirinha

3/4 oz Curaçao
1/2 oz Strega
1/4 oz Grand Marnier
2 oz Pineapple juice
Fill with Sweet and sour mix

Mixing instructions:
This is the drink, without any possible confusion, where all the drinks in the world are found, drank from every angle, please reveal this discovery to no one, have another?

Ted Berrigan's Sonnets

1 bottle Pepsi
Splash Bourbon
1 Benny
1 Pall Mall

Mixing instructions:
Crush and snort Benny, spill bourbon on floor for people who died, cigarette never leaves mouth.

Rimbaud's Drunken Boat

1 oz Absinthe makes the tart grow fonder.[1]
1 oz Absinthe makes the tongue go wander.
1 oz Absinthe makes pants go yonder.
1 oz Absinthe makes the green fairy ponder.
1 oz Absinthe makes the heart grow fondle.[2]
And the name of the star is called Wormwood: and the
    third part of the waters became wormwood; and
    many men died of the waters, because they were
    made bitter.[3]

Mixing Instructions:
The absinthe is poured into a glass (a narrow glass is best as it reduces evaporation). The spoon is filled with sugar which is then dipped into the absinthe until it is soaked. The sugar is then set alight and held over the glass until it starts to melt. It is dripped into the absinthe, which catches fire. Sound the trumpets, unleash the Drunken boats.

---

1. Ernest Dowson
2. Roxy Music
3. Revelation of St John, Chapter 8 Verse 11.

Awesome *Ezra Pound* Cake

> *My Aunt Lulu used to make the best* Ezra Pound
> *Cake in the whole world.*
> *Here is her recipe:*

Ingredients:
3 cups cake Flour
6 large Eggs
1 pound Butter
1 pound Sugar
2 teaspoons of pure Vanilla extract
1/2 teaspoon Salt
1/2 cup Buttermilk
1/2 bottle of 80 proof Dark rum
1/2 bottle of 80 proof Light rum

Mixing instructions:
Set food aside. Drink rum until you see
the apparition of these faces in the crowd;
Petals on a wet, black bough.

Kenneth Koch's Rosé, Where Did You Get That Rosé?

1 Glass of Rosé

Mixing instructions:
Oh glass of wine, how do you quench? will you teach
me?

Vladimir Mayakovsky's Cloud in Trousers

2 oz Vodka
1 sodden Brain
1 bloated Lackey
1 greasy Couch
1 bloody morsel of Heart
Equal amounts Grapefruit and cranberry juice

Mixing instructions:
Grow irreproachably tender: not a man,
but a cloud in trousers!

Lewis Carroll's Jabberwocky Juice

1-1/2 oz Rum (your preference)
1 Slithy tove
2 oz Pineapple juice
1 Gyre
1 Gimble
2 oz Cream of coconut
Pinch of Wabe
Hint of Jubjub
1/2 Tumtum sprig

Mixing instructions:
Set the vorpal blade to snicker-snack, galumph, chortle,
serve in a cocktail glass over Outgrabe.

Robert Burns' Bottle and an Honest Friend

1 Bottle Macallan
1 Bottle Glennfiddich
1 Bottle Glenlivet
1 Bottle Highland Park

Mixing instructions:
Have Single Malt Scotch Tasting Slam while singing:
There's nane that's blest of human kind,
But the cheerful and the gay, man,
Fal, la, la, &c.

Here's a bottle and an honest friend!
What wad ye wish for mair, man?
Wha kens, before his life may end,
What his share may be o' care, man?

Then catch the moments as they fly,
And use them as ye ought, man:
Believe me, happiness is shy,
And comes not aye when sought, man.

The *Rumi*

1 Huge barrel of Wine
0 cups